COOKING GREEK WITH DAPHNE

COOKING GREEK WITH DAPHNE

ALLAN KONYA WITH DAPHNE VLOUMIDI

Archimedia Press Limited

2020

Published in the United Kingdom in 2020
by Archimedia Press Limited, Weavers Cottage
Clay Lane, Beenham, Reading RG7 5PA

British Library Cataloguing-in-Publication Data
A catalogue record for this title is available from the British Library.

Library of Congress Cataloguing-in-Publication Data. A catalogue record for this title is available from the Library of Congress.

ISBN 978-1-9162425-1-7

Manufactured in the USA, the UK and Australia by Lightning Source.

To Iannis, Daphne and the Votsala family
for the happy times spent with them all .

Table of Contents

Introduction

Over the years my wife Sonia and I have travelled a great deal in Greece. Firstly, many visits to Mykonos for me to further my studies into spirit of place, and then later to various parts of the country for Sonia to learn as much as possible about the traditional weaving. A great deal was discovered in various places and Crete, the largest of the islands, was an absolute treasure trove. Because of this we thought that Lesvos, the third largest island, must also be worth a visit. However, we found this difficult to plan because we usually stayed in the main town of the area or island but could not find anywhere in Mytilini that appealed to us. Then, by chance, I read somewhere about Votsala Hotel that was located in a very calm and quiet area on the beach of Thermi, about 11km from the centre of town and where, amongst other good things, classical music was played while one enjoyed breakfast under the trees on the waterside terrace.

We learned from the website that in the 1990s, after spending many years in Athens, Iannis and his wife Daphne took over the hotel that was built by his father in the 1960s. It went on to say that Iannis, an architect, had brought Votsala into the 21st century while maintaining the charm of the past. Ten years ago they bought an old stone pension a five minutes' walk away that Iannis has converted and transformed into what is now called Villa Daphnis and Chloe. This operates as a family orientated facility during the school holidays, functions as the base for spring walks and other special events, and also makes an ideal place for hosting retreats, seminars, workshops, weddings and family reunions.

. Inspired by all of this we made a short

Votsala hotel seen from the sea.

The wonderful varied buffet breakfast with various special homemade dishes.

Enjoying breakfast at a waterside table.

visit to the island at the start of the 2006 season while things were still very quiet. While we immediately liked Iannis and his hotel very much we were not particularly impressed with the little we saw of the island and nor did we find any weavers. So, we more or less decided that we would not be returning to Lesvos.

For some unknown reason I happened to look at the hotel's website early in 2008 and saw that they were promoting cooking classes with Daphne and Eleni on Sundays in July and August. In addition to this, in June and September they were having "Taste of Greece" — one-week seminars it said that offered "the possibility to join a more intensive programme focussed on Greek eating and drinking culture." In spite of the decision we took some years earlier we found this very tempting and ended up back at Votsala in September.

This is when we met Daphne and her cousin Eleni (a dentist from Athens) who led the week of food-related activities. In addition to the cooking classes there were visits to an ouzo distillery, an olive oil museum, and a traditional 19th century house in Petra where, under a large magnolia tree in the garden, vegetables we had collected from a local grower were prepared and turned into tasty dishes that we enjoyed for lunch after which Daphne read us a story about her childhood. In the afternoon we spent some time in Molyvos, Sykaminia and Mandamados on the way back to Votsala. There were various other visits including one to the attractive mountain village of Agiassos.

The experiences we were privileged to enjoy during this holiday led us to develop a great fondness, and in some cases love, for Lesvos, Daphne and Iannis, for the Votsala Hotel, and the delightful 'family' of lovely, friendly people who keep it all functioning so well. We have subsequently enjoyed a number of happy, relaxed and informal holidays there, meeting and making many friends most of whom are regulars and have been for a number of years.

Over the years we have participated in most of the wonderfully interesting non-compulsory afternoon walks in various parts of the island that Iannis organizes. These usually end in a taverna with all the participants enjoying a communal meal of traditional Greek food.

On Saturday evenings we have enjoyed the legendary Votsala buffet-style barbecues — that even vegetarians love because of the large selection of wonderful salads — and on Sunday afternoons we have participated in further cooking classes with Daphne and Nina, one of the receptionists at the hotel.

It is the food from these classes, as well as the Saturday barbecues and Wednesday evening meals, that form the basis for the recipes in this book. There are some additional recipes that we have enjoyed at various places over the years, and I have taken the liberty of including these in Appendix 1 to make the distinction clear. No attempt has been made to produce 'arty' or 'posed' photographs of the food. Most of the illustrations are photographs taken while the food was being prepared during the cooking classes, and of the final products before they were eaten for the meal afterwards.

Votsala is not a luxury hotel: the rooms are simple but attractive and all have a balcony overlooking the garden and the sea. For more information see the many complimentary reviews on TripAdvisor, as well as their own instructive website at: www.votsalahotel.com

Daphne

Daphne Vloumidi, our Daphne, was born in Athens in 1956. In her book 'Nostimo'— which means 'tasty' in Greek — she shares both nostalgic stories and her recipes and gives the assurance that the dishes are "poly nostimo" (very tasty). She describes how in her youth she would wait impatiently for the summer to come. They were always the same and spent on Lesvos in the large old house of her grandmother and her godmother (the grandmother's sister) in Petra, where she would spend three whole months. The daily walks in the garden with her godmother would end by them resting on a bench where she would be told stories that she enjoyed.

This explains briefly the origin of Daphne's connection to Lesvos but does not really tell one anything about this rather special, humble and gentle lady who spends from April to October each year on the island helping Iannis run the hotel. In 2012 together with a German friend she founded Odysseas, a non-profit organisation that provides learning and integration projects for young refugees housed in camps on the island. They try to help these people make good use of their time on Lesvos and, after the dangers of their trip, find a way into the future.

In recognition of this work, in 2018 Daphne was honoured by Gariwo (Gardens of the Righteous Worldwide), who are a non-profit organisation in service of memory. Its aim is to heighten awareness and interest in the figures and the tales of the Righteous, women and men who fought and are still fighting in defence of human dignity. The term *Righteous* comes from the Bible, which states that "whoever saves a life saves the whole world" and it was applied for the first time in Israel with reference to those who rescued Jews from Nazi persecution in Europe. On 24 January 2003 a garden was inaugurated at Monte Stella Hill, Milan, that is dedicated to the Righteous worldwide. Every year new wild cherry trees are planted in honour of, and symbolically representing, those selected during a ceremony in the presence of the Righteous themselves or of their relatives, and a memorial plaque is placed in the meadow below.

In her speech at the ceremony Daphne referred to the widely reported refugee problems on Lesvos in 2015 "… then, you do the obvious. You help in any way and at any price. And there are so many things to do. You also believed that you knew just what to do, you who in the past, have been in touch with so many refugees, you who have eaten, laughed, heard all those painful stories, you who have shared so much time with them, so you think that this time you will do it again, you will not bend, you will not be desperate. You are strong and you know. And suddenly the truth slaps you in the face. You are tired, desperate, you cry. You feel that all your efforts are nothing more than a drop in the ocean.

"I tell you the truth: that is how I felt. Although I still had my faith and my dream for a better world, my motivation was the real daily needs of all these thousands of people who came to our island, not to have a holiday, but to be saved from the death that was waiting for them outside their homes. It was also all of you, and I thank you from the bottom of my heart for the honour you give me today and I share it with all those who have supported me enormously, working together with solidarity in that difficult period of the refugee-crisis: my family, my friends and many others, local population and tourists."

Related to all of this and based on her feeling of seeing so many small children who had made such a difficult journey arriving on the island, Daphne has recently written a children's book, titled *Quilombo the Scruffy Little Elephant*, which was shortlisted in Greece for a literature prize. It was originally written as a letter to their granddaughter who was living in England at the time, and it has lessons for all of us about inclusion and difference. Quilombo is a small elephant who arrives in 2015 on the island of Lesvos from a distant land. Dirty and abandoned, he seems foreign and different. But he's just the same as all the children in the world, those living in refugee camps, and those sleeping peacefully in their homes with toy animals in their arms.

Finally, to get back to food and cooking: in the epilogue of her book *Nostimo* Daphne writes "When you think a cookbook is something trivial, you suddenly discover that the essence is not in the recipes, but in the human relationships that developed over time at 'Votsala'…"I remembered summer scenes, warm, encouraging talks, children's eyes staring at me in their effort to learn to cook…and re-enjoyed the lazy time we spent eating… what we had cooked together".

Below: Iannis and Daphne at the Votsala Hotel - they and all their staff do everything they can to make your stay enjoyable, relaxing and interesting. Nothing is ever too much trouble."

Above: with the mayor of Milan who unveiled the plaque honouring her. Below: the cover of Daphne's book for children.

Mediterranean diet

The importance of the Mediterranean diet consists in the fact that there is a general consensus among health professionals — after considerable research — that this diet is healthy and leads to notably low incidence of chronic diseases (cancers, coronary heart disease, and diabetes) and to high life expectancy rates. The diet is characterized by abundant plant foods (fruits, mainly as typical daily desserts, vegetables, bread, other forms of cereals, beans, nuts and seeds). It also includes olive oil as the principle source of fat, moderate amounts of dairy products (principally cheese and yogurt), low to moderate amounts of fish and poultry, red meat in low amounts, and wine consumed in low to moderate quantities, normally with meals

If there is evidence that one particular version of the diet is somewhat better than the others, the Cretan would be it, probably because it has retained its authenticity, and the innumerable articles and books published in recent years testifies to this.

Another island that has attracted much attention in recent years is Ikaria, situated in the Aegean Sea south west of Samos. Ikaria looks similar to any number of other Greek islands. But there is one vital difference: people here live much longer than the population on other islands and on the mainland. In fact, people here live on average 10 years longer than those in the rest of Europe and America — around one in three Ikarians lives into their 90s. Although the diet is similar to the Mediterranean diet found elsewhere in Greece, there are also differences. A cardiologist who was part of the University of Athens research team, found that the Ikarian diet featured a lot of beans and not much meat or refined sugar. The locals also feast on locally grown and wild greens, some of which contain 10 times more antioxidants than are found in red wine, as well as potatoes and goat's milk.

The Ikarians drink a lot of herb tea and small quantities of coffee; daily calorie consumption is not high. Ikaria is still an isolated island, without tourists, which means that, especially in the villages in the north, where the highest longevity rates have been recorded, life is largely unaffected by the westernised way of living. Research also suggests that it is not only diet but a number of subtly powerful, mutually enhancing and pervasive factors that are at work. For example, the Ikarian habit of taking afternoon naps may help extend life, and social structure is probably an important factor. Although it is a slightly austere environment where life has traditionally required hard work it is also a very social one. At the heart of the island's social scene are the series of 24-hour festivals, known as *panigyri*, which all age groups attend. Family is also a vital part of Ikarian culture and most older people have children and grandchildren actively involved in their lives.

Until around the mid-1960s Greeks lived by the seasons. Not having refrigerators they pickled and preserved vegetables, and smoked or salted fish and meat for leaner periods. In addition to this, good Christians observed the main fasting periods imposed by the Orthodox Church, and obeyed the restrictions on meat, dairy products, eggs and fish with blood every Wednesday and Friday throughout the year. Modern Greeks however are eating less and less of the traditional food and abandoning their culinary roots in favour of more and more processed and delivered food. As a result cases of cancer, heart disease, diabetes and obesity have become more prominent.

Traditional Greek food

What — one can ask — is traditional Greek food? To start with it is simple, earthy [or would rustic be a better word?], wholesome and unpretentious. One could almost call it unfashionable in the sense that like the Italians, Greeks generally seem to prefer homemade fare rather than so-called creative cooking produced by a celebrity chef in a deluxe restaurant. Nowadays, however, as a result of their newfound wealth, and accompanying obsession with social prestige, this is sadly not always true.

The traditional dishes as well as being delicious are some of the healthiest as they rely enormously on seasonal vegetables— a specific vegetable always implies a season — and, in winter, on pulses. Although Greeks consume a great deal of fat it is almost never animal fat or seed oils, but sweet virgin olive oil balanced very often by the acidity of lemon juice. Added to this are garlic and herbs. The flavour comes from the purity and freshness of these ingredients with piquant spices seldom, if ever, being used. Greek Food is often strongly related to the rituals, folklore and celebrations that are so important in the daily life of the people.

Greeks are passionate about their food and for them freshness of the ingredients is a primary consideration, almost a mania. One of the great tragedies of what we call progress is that while the variety of fruit and vegetables in our supermarkets and hypermarkets has never been greater, the food is becoming increasingly mass-produced. Quantity is very often more important than quality, and even when quality is considered it has to do with size and shape, which can be sold, rather than flavour and nutritive value which cannot. Picked most often before it matures, transported for hundreds or thousands of kilometres, and sometimes kept in storage, produce may be weeks old before it reaches the shelves. So, in addition to nutrients, flavour and texture are lost. As a result of all this the taste of properly sun-ripened fruit or truly fresh vegetables is rapidly becoming a figment of the imagination. Fortunately, this is still not true of much of the food in Greece.

Food for the Greeks is not simply a biological necessity, but is very much intertwined with their lives, forming a part of virtually every important event, both private and communal, from the time they are born to beyond the grave. Until fairly recently most Greeks adhered to the rhythms of fasting, determined by the strict rules of the Orthodox Church, and feasting which punctuates the forced deprivation with a joyful excess. This together with past poverty, is the reason for the large number of vegetarian dishes found here. The simple, down to earth, unsophisticated food reflects the Greeks' rural peasant background, with recipes and techniques having been passed down from generation to generation. So, while everyone knows the traditional food, and how it varies with the seasons and the religious calendar, every Greek cook has his or her own particular version of each classic dish.

The recipes in this book are, according to Daphne, simple and easy. She goes on to say that recipes she thinks easy may seem complicated, but she will show her own way of cooking which she has "ensured is simple and fast, so that this daily process does not become a source of torment…you should not be afraid of mistakes. I don't know how and why, however, in some magical way the food usually comes out quite tasty."

The elements of Greek food

Here follows a description of the main ingredients that will be found in, or may accompany, many of the recipes in this book. Some, such as olives for example, are often served by themselves as mezes.

Olives

Since antiquity the olive tree has a permanent presence in the landscape of Greece, and in the daily life and customs of its people. The culture of the olive tree and its products deeply influenced the civilization of ancient and modern Greeks and has played an important role not only in the economy of the country, but in all aspects of Greek civilization — historical, folkloric, traditional, medicinal and artistic. In one of his poems Odysseus Elytis wrote that "If you deconstruct Greece, you will in the end see an olive tree, a grape vine and a boat remain."

The olive belongs to the family of trees and shrubs Oleaceae which includes Lilac, true Jasmine, Forsythia and Privet. Olives and olive oil come from the true olive, Olea europaea; although not indigenous it spread throughout the Mediterranean at least 6000 years ago.

One valuable source confirming the importance of the olive tree and its fruits for the ancient Greeks is the evidence provided by the Linear B sun-dried clay tablets unearthed at the palaces of Knossos on Crete, and at Pylos on the mainland. Linear B has roughly 200 symbols, divided into syllabic signs with phonetic values and ideograms with semantic values. The tablets, dating back as far as about 1450 BC, formed part of the archives of these Mycenaean palaces and differentiate between the olive tree, the crop and the oil each being depicted by a different ideogram.

A variety of olives and a bottle of olive oil.

The hardy evergreen olive tree takes about 8 years to produce its first crop, and then generally only bears a high yield of fruit every second year unless well irrigated. These trees are most productive after between 60 and 100 years and live for centuries with a normal life-span of around 5 or 6 centuries. There are a number of varieties in Greece that produce edible fruits with a great diversity of flavours. The different flavours and textures of the fruit are not only dependent on the variety but also to some extent on the region from which they come, as well as on the degree of ripeness when picked and on the curing method used. The best known abroad are the commonly available almond-shaped Kalamata olives that are black, green or purple depending on the stage of ripeness when they are picked. They enjoy Protected Designation of Origin status.

Olive Oil

The olive, because of its high oil content and good preservation qualities, was in antiquity a very important concentrated food, particularly useful for periods of scarcity and long voyages on land and sea. For the ancient Greeks olive oil was — it seems — present in most cooked dishes, whether they were fried, marinated or basted in it or served with a sauce for which it was the vehicle. It was sometimes an ingredient in bread-making, and, in a plain snack, was sometimes the only relish that helped one's bread to go down, for butter, which can serve a similar purpose for us, was scarcely used. In fact someone who ate butter was considered by them to be a barbarian.

So valuable was the olive oil that Homer called it "liquid gold," and indeed its uses were many. Not only did it form the basis of one of the healthiest diets found anywhere, but athletes and warriors rubbed it into their skin; as fuel it provided light and heat; and medicines, cosmetics and soaps were made from it. Then, as now, virtually no part of the olive tree or its fruit was discarded: the leaves were used in treating boils and ulcers or fed to animals; the beautifully patterned wood was carved into small implements and decorative objects; charcoal was made from the pruned branches; and even the discarded piths were used as fertilizer and fuel. Today the olive tree continues to be utilized in nearly the same ways as it was in ancient times.

Olive oil is much used in the sacraments and rituals of the Greek Orthodox Church. For example, when babies are baptized they are anointed with olive oil. In some parts of the country, unbaptized children are referred to as *aladot*i — unoiled or unanointed. In the marriage sacrament, one of the prayers for the newlywed couple is that their home never be without bread or oil, the two most basic foods, the two foods from which one can always find nourishment. In the Orthodox Church however, olive oil is not consumed during lent or penance while Orthodox monks use it sparingly in their diet. Exceptions are on feast days and Sundays.

Like wine, no two olive oils are exactly alike. Each oil is distinct, with the flavour, bouquet or aroma, and often the colour being determined by factors such as soil quality and composition, climate, and of course the olive variety. Altitude, the olive grove's exposure to sunlight, how the olives are grown and harvested, how ripe the fruit is when collected, the time taken between gathering and pressing, the type of press — old style hydraulic or the new centrifugal — are also factors that have an effect on the quality.

The finest quality oil, known as 'extra virgin' is produced simply by crushing fresh, cold, first-grade olives; no heating or other processing is involved. It is tested and if it contains no more than 0.8% acidity, it is considered extra virgin grade oil and is judged to have a superior taste. Extra virgin olive oil accounts for less than 10% of oil in many producing countries; the percentage is far higher in the Mediterranean countries and in Greece is up to 80%. In some areas of Greece olives are pressed before they ripen, producing *agourelaio*, literally 'unripe olive oil', also a very pure extra virgin oil from the first pressing. It has a distinctive intense, fruity yet also sharp and slightly spicy flavour.

***Fyllo* (pastry)**

Fyllo (also spelled *fillo* and *phyllo*), which means leaf in Greece, is paper-thin translucent sheets of dough used, with several layers together to strengthen the delicate sheets, to make a large variety of savoury pies such as the well-known *spanakopitta* (spinach) and *tyropitta* (cheese), and sweet pastries such as *baklava.* Although an integral part of Greek cuisine, it is also commonly used in the Middle East and the Balkans.

Not so long ago every Greek housewife

made her own thin sheets of *fyllo* and there are innumerable recipes for the dough which is fairly simple to make: typically a mixture of flour, water, olive oil, salt and, often, something acidic such as vinegar or lemon juice. But rolling out the pastry is another matter needing time, patience and practice, and it is amazing to watch the women do this on their special round boards with thin, about 500 mm long, perfectly straight rolling pins.

Until very recently it was possible to find places where *fyllo* was made by hand. For example, in a small shop behind the central market in Chania on Crete. After being mixed in a mangle-like piece of equipment, the dough was weighed out and formed into balls. After a short period of resting these were rolled out into flat disks and then the fascinating bit started. Each disk was rotated rapidly and expertly by hand so that it became thinner and thinner, and bigger and bigger until it was thrown onto the centre of a large table covered with a coarse linen cloth. As it landed it entrapped the air and formed a dome - all great fun and very dramatic. It was then stretched by being gently pulled and coaxed on all sides towards the edges of the table. After it had been trimmed and had dried it was finally cut into equal sized pieces that were floured and stacked on top of each other.

Sadly, the art of making fyllo has been lost and the old-fashioned fyllo makers are unfortunately disappearing, as they are threatened (even in Greece) by the growing popularity of the frozen variety that is commercially produced by machine.

Feta

Feta is a type of Greek cheese with a Protected Designation of Origin status traditionally made predominantly from sheep's milk although it may contain up to

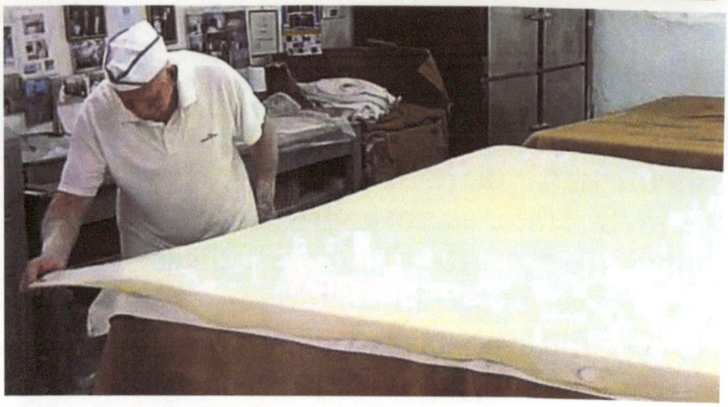

Top & above: the rotated dough is thrown onto a table and then stretched to all the edges.

Below: homemade fyllo using the traditional long wooden rolling pin.

30% of goats' milk. The defining characteristic of feta cheese is that it is brined or pickled, which gives it a salty, tangy flavor and a crumbly consistency.

It is a simple, wholesome cheese, the result of pasteurized whole milk which is separated into curds and whey by means of a curdling agent – usually rennet. Rennet is derived from the membrane of the stomachs of unweaned animals and contains rennin, an enzyme that coagulates milk. Rennin is also found in the juices of some plants, such as figs, artichokes and clover.

After the milk has been heated, cooled and curdled, the solids rise to the top. They are removed and placed in baskets or thin cheesecloth bags that strain out the remainder of the whey. The 'heads' of cheese are cut into pieces (*fetes*), salted, and placed in wooden barrels, large square metal containers (*dochia*), or (occasionally) in the age-old manner, in skin bags, and left in a cool place to ripen. Cheese-making begins in September and continues throughout the winter, culminating in spring when the animals give birth and their milk is at its richest.

Feta is not always the same and there can be great differences not only in appearance but also in taste. These differences are dependent chiefly on the type and quality of the milk used and its fat content. Sheep and goat's milk have a higher fat content than cow's milk and its richness can vary according to the quantity and quality of what the animals eat. Since almost 90% of Greek animals are allowed to forage freely in rugged mountain terrain, they are obviously not always consuming the same plants. Bitter herbs will cause bitter milk, and sweet herbs, sweet milk — and thus bitter or sweet cheese. Other factors, such as the kind and amount of rennet used, the temperature of the milk, and the length of time and conditions under which the cheese is stored, also affect the final product.

Barrel feta (*varelisia*), which is generally of the medium (*metrio*) type, comprises most of the feta sold in Greece. White and crumbly, it is neither soft nor hard, and not too tangy: a good all-purpose cheese for almost every taste. Hard (*skliri*) feta is the saltiest and most sharp tasting of the barrel fetas, indicating that it has been ripened in brine for a longer time. It is the least likely to spoil. Feta that is too salty for one's taste can be soaked in milk or water for several hours, or even days, changing the milk or water bath frequently.

Tinned feta (*dochio*), generally from the various regions of Northern Greece, comprises some of the best and most consistent quality feta. An excellent choice is that from Dodoni. This type resembles the cheese made by the nomadic Vlach shepherds who once roamed the high mountain ranges of the Balkan peninsula. One of the oldest types of feta still being made, principally in Central Greece and Southern Evia, is called *touloumotiri*. It takes its name from the fact that the cheese was originally stored in goatskins turned inside out. The contact of the cheese with the bacteria in the animal's hair gave it a characteristic flavour similar to blue cheese but without the mould.

Greeks are very particular about their feta. Some like it soft and moist and rather mild, others prefer it as hard and crumbly as it can be made. Others want the distinct flavour of the goat-hide while still others prefer it to be lemony-sour. Although the differences are subtle, most Greek cheese shops and markets sell at least a dozen types.

Feta is the quintessential Greek table cheese but it is used in innumerable ways. It is, for example, an important part of the well-known Greek salad and is a major ingredient in the popular traditional *fyllo* pies such as *spanakopita* (spinach pie) and *tyropita* (cheese pie). It is almost always served with a whole family of foods in Greece known as *lathera* (stews gently simmered in olive oil until soft). In some places the cheese is mixed into the stewpot until it melts and melds with the vegetables, forming a creamy, luscious sauce.

Above: slices of typical feta cheese.
Below: as a main ingredient of a Greek salad.

Feta cheese is usually sold packed in water or sometimes oil. Since it will dry out if removed from the water for too long, it's a good idea to store it in the water it was packed in, or rinse it and store it in fresh water, ideally in a ceramic or glass container (never metal) loosely covered in a way that allows it to breathe.

Graviera

Produced in several areas, this is one of the best Greek table cheeses. Sheep's milk graviera is made on Crete — the best known area for this cheese and with Protected Denomination of Origin (PDO) as is the Agrafon graviera. It is also produced in Mytilini, Dodoni, Arta and Kalpaki. Made in wheels, the rind of this hard cheese is marked with the characteristic crisscross pattern of its draining cloth. With a light yellow colour, it may contain a few small holes, even a horizontal crack or two, and has a mellow, slightly sweet and nutty taste.

Cow's milk graviera, which is yellower and a little creamier, is made mostly on Tinos, Naxos (also PDO), Syros and Corfu amongst other places. One of the reasons this cheese is so popular is that, like feta, it can be used in many different ways: as a table cheese, for saganaki, in cooked dishes (especially au gratin), and for grating.

Ladotyri

This is a hard cheese made of sheep's and goat's milk in the shape of miniature barrels. The name translates as 'olive oil cheese' - *lado* (olive oil) and *tyri* (cheese) — referring to the fact that the cheese is traditionally steeped in olive oil and ripened for a minimum of three months. A major advantage of this is that the cheese has a very long life without refrigeration, considerably longer than a brine cheese like feta for example. Ladotyri Mytilinis is produced on Lesvos with POD.

Tomatoes may not look 'perfect' but are bursting with wonderful flavour and texture.

Vegetables and fruit

Vegetables have a huge impact on Greek food, as with many other Mediterranean countries. Traditionally and up to the mid-1960s, Greeks tended to utilize what was in season — tomatoes and aubergines (egg-plant) in summer, cabbage and leeks in winter, and artichokes in spring. Until very recently one of the main influences on what was eaten at various times was the fasting periods throughout the year of the Orthodox Church that were observed by most Greeks.

Greece is blessed with a wide gamut of basic ingredients that flourish in this perfect Mediterranean climate. Fruits, greens, and a wide array of fresh, seasonal vegetables and legumes are the mainstay of traditional Greek cooking, some with distinctly regional associations. As Diana Kochilas writes in her book *The Greek Vegetarian:* "Greek cooking, with few exceptions, has always sprung from the garden...(it) boasts myriad recipes for vegetables, legumes, greens and grains, in endless combinations that call for little embellishment beyond olive oil, salt, and the refreshing, enhancing juice of the lemon. Meat has never played a primary role...The backbone of the cuisine has always been what is harvested, in either wild or cultivated form."

The whole Mediterranean fruit bowl grows in temperate Greece and each season has its specialties.

Greeks, in keeping with the Mediterranean tradition, typically eat several servings of fruit a day, mainly after the meal.

Above: lemons are a must in any Greek kitchen; they are a basic ingredient and add the sour element to many dishes from soups to puddings. It is squeezed on everything from potatoes to meats, on roasted and fried cheeses, and adds a classic Greek taste to vegetables and fish.

Below: of all the fruits in the Mediterranean garden, the pomegranate, with its serrated crown-like calyx, its coarse ruddy skin, and honeycomb of blood-coloured beads within, is one of the most ancient and mythical. It is found everywhere in Greece and the fruit is deeply embedded in Greek culture. They are considered auspicious symbols of good luck, fertility and abundance.

Herbs (*votana*)
Greece is famous for its unique herbs and spices, so it is not surprising that in Greek cuisine the use of herbs plays a major role — their fragrance permeates every island. Herbs grow profusely in Greece. They grow as a wild carpet of the forests, the scrublands and mountains on most islands, and many people pick what they need from these shrubby native plants and grow their own pots of vital herbs like basil, thyme, oregano and mint on windowsills, patios and terraces.

The excellent quality and the number of herbs and spice-producing plants that grow naturally in Greece reflect the country's long periods of sunshine and the variability of its landscape. This special landscape makes Greek flora so rich, that of the 7500 different species of plants growing in Greece, 850 of them are found only there.

Herbs are loved all over Greece and many widely used today have been part of the Greek culture, and essentials in the diet for many thousands of years, with most still having Latin names derived from ancient Greek. In very early times the most notable uses of herbs and spices were in medicine, in the making of holy oils and unguents, and as aphrodisiacs. Priests employed them in worship, incantations, and rituals. Hippocrates (460-370 BC), the Greek 'father of medicine' employed them in his everyday practice.

From spring to autumn every Greek family that is able to will combine outings to the countryside with gathering the available herbs, depending on the time of the year. At the correct time the stems are cut and gathered into a bunch that is tied together and hung upside down to dry out exposed to the heat of the sun but protected from damp or rain. When dry enough the leaves and flowers are crumbled over a sheet of paper, and then stored in a jar for the winter.
Among the most common herbs found in the countryside is rosemary (*dendrolivano*), which is used sparingly. Sage (*faskomilo*) is present all over the mountains and its smell is overpowering. It is usually used in a tea, although it is claimed to have soothing and healing properties for various ailments. Mint (*diosmos*) is used to flavour *keftedes* (meatballs) and in some pies and salads. Basil (*vassilikos*) grows incredibly well due to the climate and is actually only now becoming popular in various dishes because traditionally Greeks grow basil for good luck or ornamentally, and it is often found in a pot on a window sill. They say that it also chases away the persistent mosquito! Dill (*anitho*) is used in *pitas* (pies), salads and *dolmadas*. Parsley (*maidanos*) is used as a garnish as well as in some meat and vegetable dishes. Bay leaves (*dafnofila*) are used in some soups and stews. *Selino* is actually wild celery and is used in some stews, particularly the *hirino* (pork) with celery which is served in the winter. Also much used are fennel (*maratho*), coriander (*koriandroto*) and chamomile (*hamomili*) mainly used as a tisane (herbal tea). As Rena Salaman explains "I do not think there has been a Greek baby that at some point in his or her life has not been quietened down and sent to sleep with the magical weak infusion of chamomile flowers, considered in Greece to be a mother's ally".

However, the most indispensable of Greek herbs are the two primary ones used in all cooking, thyme (*thymari*) and oregano (*rigani*), that grow in a number of varieties. Picked at the right time, dried and stored, they lose none of their beautiful scent and can be used throughout the year. When dried *thymari* is the only herb that neither loses nor alters its aroma, while *rigani* to the contrary seems to develop a more concentrated scent and flavour when dried. Beautifully aromatic this is the Greek herb par excellence and it is used as a vital seasoning to enhance the flavor of grilled meats and casseroles that contain tomatoes. It is also used to season cheese, egg dishes, salads, dressings, stews, meatballs, pasta and vegetables.

SPICES AND FLAVOURINGS

Spices were in use in the Mediterranean from around 3000 BC, when they were brought by caravans from Asia and Africa. Originally used for medicine, embalming, and as perfumes they were soon used in the cooking of food and flavouring of wine.

Greek cooking does not rely on a large variety of herbs and spices but the combination of a few — very few. The food is generally not spicy and not heavily seasoned. The focus is on the vegetables, bread, fish and meat and the philosophy seems to be bringing out the natural flavour of these things rather than hide it or disguise it with spices.

Salt (*alati*) is the most basic ingredient and Greek cooking relies heavily on it to bring out the flavour of meat, fish and vegetables, and most of the salt used is from the sea. There are also many places in the country where salt is harvested on flat plains by the sea and it is of a high quality.

In Greek folklore salt has great purifying powers and can be used to ward off demons and evil spirits, simply by throwing it over one's left shoulder. It can also be used to get rid of an unwanted human presence. If there is an unwelcome visitor in the house who one wants to leave, all that one needs to do is sprinkle salt behind them. The powers of the salt will chase the person out, but care must be taken to ensure that the guest does not see this because if he or she does then the power of the salt is weakened. It is also customary to sprinkle salt in a new house before occupying it because the salt will drive out any evil that may affect one and one's family.

Pepper (*peperi*) which like salt is found on every table. The pungent black pepper is generally preferred to the stronger, less subtle white

Cinnamon (*kanela*) is a heady spice, obtained from the inner bark of several trees from the genus *Cinnamomum,* and is used to maximum advantage in the Greek kitchen for both sweet and savoury foods. It is a favourite flavouring for lamb dishes and is used in many sauces, biscuits and pies. It is also sprinkled on slices of apples and pears for a desert after a big meal.

Cloves *(garifalo)* are an important ingredient in *stifado* and are also inserted into pork before it is roasted. Cloves are often used in cakes, pastries, and sweets, including *kourambiedes*, traditional Christmas cookies. It can be used in its whole-seed form, grated into soups, or as part of seasoning for meat, fish, poultry, or vegetables.

Cumin *(kumino)* is used in *soutzoukakia*, the spicey meatballs served in tomato sauce.

Mastic (mastikha) is a gum-like resin obtained from the evergreen shrub or small tree called Skhinos (Pistacia lentiscus) that grows between 1.5 m to 3.5 m tall on the island of Chios. Within the EU mastic production on Chios is granted protected Designation of Origin (PDO) which is the equivalent of appellation systems used throughout the world. This is granted because, although the tree is native to the whole Mediterranean region, only the variety Chia which is grown in the 24 villages and communities known as *'Mastikhahoria'* (literally 'the mastic villages') in the south of the island, 'weep' the resin when their bark is scored. Here the aromatic, ivory coloured sap is also known as 'Chios tears.'

As a spice mastic is unique because it is so versatile, insinuating itself with equal facility into sweet and savoury dishes, and pairing beautifully with everything from citrus to tomatoes to chocolate to creams and yogurt. In order to use it one must first crush it in a mortar and pestle, either with a little salt (for savoury dishes) or sugar (for sweet dishes).

Nutmeg (*moschokarido*), is one of the prime ingredients in the quintessential Greek dish of moussaka, it is key in *pastitsio*, a pasta dish made with ground beef and a bechamel sauce. But, the Greeks use it also in all sorts of dishes, from desserts to sauces and liqueurs.

Saffron — Greek red saffron (*Krokos kozanis*) — is a spice derived from the dried stigmas of the saffron crocus (Crocus sativus), and has throughout history remained among the world's most costly substances. With its bitter taste, hay-like fragrance, and slight metallic notes it has been used as a seasoning, fragrance, dye, and medicine. Although native to Southwest Asia it was first cultivated in Greece.

A small quantity of this spice — it should be used sparingly — adds a subtle spicy flavour, a lovely golden colour, and a delicate aroma to one's dishes. To use it, a few threads are infused in a cup of hot water and the coloured liquid added towards the end of cooking, or the threads are crumbled, and add directly to the pot. Alternatively, they may be dry roasted, crumbled and then steeped in liquid. Unlike other spices, a good pinch will suffice to add flavour and colour in most dishes. It is commonly used in rice-based recipes and dishes.

Sesame seeds (*sousami*). The sesame plant produces numerous seed pods that measure up to 2 - 3 centimetres in length. When they are ripe, they pop open at the tip — hence the expression 'open sesame' — and release small, flat, oval seeds. The main varieties grown today, however, have been cultivated to produce seed pods that do not pop so that they can be gathered with a combine harvester and mechanically cleaned afterwards. The seeds differ in size, colour, and thickness of husk, according to their variety. Oil, protein and carbohydrates are the main ingredients and the high energy it provides is mainly due to its oil. Sesame contains a small quantity of carbohydrates, but a rather high quantity of dietary fibres and is particularly rich in calcium, phosphorus and iron.

Although Greece is only a small producer of sesame seed it has the largest apparent consumption in the EU. The seeds are used on breads and in halva and with honey to make a sweet called *pasteli*.

Vinegar (*ksidhi*) has been used in some form since Ancient times and is still being used in Greek cuisine. Because of its rich winemaking tradition, the most common type of vinegar that can be found in Greece is wine vinegar. Although most Greek salads are primarily dressed with olive oil and herbs such as oregano, some people do sprinkle some wine vinegar on their salads if they have it handy. However, it's mainly used in many popular Greek dishes such as *tzatziki*, lentil soup, seafood dishes, and *skordalia*. It is especially used in dishes that don't involve the use of tomato or lemon, which also provide a level of acidity to a dish.

Quince (*kydoni*)

An apple-like fruit, its Latin botanical name cydonia vulgaris reveals its ancient Greek root, *kydoni*, that is also the modern Greek word for both the tree and the fruit, which

Above: quinces on a market stall in winter.

have been around in this part of the world for thousands of years.

Autumn is the season for this odd-looking, lumpy, yellowish-green fruit, usually covered with a thin fuzz. The flesh is hard, gritty and astringent and needs long cooking to become edible. The point of ripeness is elusive. If one waits until it gets soft, the flesh gets mushy and loses its aroma so they are usually picked when they are not too green, but not entirely yellow — firm and as free from blemishes as possible. The delicate perfume of unripe quinces is unmistakable, and these are best for culinary purposes.

It is used in some meat dishes — pork, chicken or veal stewed with quince, spices, tomato sauce, and sometimes vegetables. It is also baked or poached, often in sweet Mavrodaphne wine, as a dessert and this is often found being served in tavernas during the winter.

Garlic (*skordo*)

Garlic is widely used and is an essential ingredient for example in *tzatziki* as well as in many baked dishes. *Skordalia* is a strong garlic sauce, made with either bread or potato, and served with fried cod amongst other things.

Pulses (legumes)

The family of pulses includes beans, lentils, chickpeas, fava beans, peas etc. and are generally regarded as the crops harvested solely for the dry seed rather than those used as vegetables or mainly grown for oil extraction. What characterises them is high nutritional value and that they are a rich source of composite slow-absorption carbohydrates, amino-acids, natural fibres, vitamins (B, C and E), trace elements and of course, proteins. Pulses have zero fat and sugar, and they are an integral part of the broader Mediterranean diet. They have always been essential to the Greek table.

Andrew Dalby writes in his history of food in Greece that a form of lentils and wild peas were being not only collected, but actually encouraged, if not cultivated, in Greece before 7000 BC. Around 6000 BC new cooking methods became available and the appearance of pottery around that time meant the possibility of cooking by boiling which led to the invention — as far as Greece is concerned — of those favourite, cheap and practical foods of later times, gruel, porridge and pulse soups. In classical times some pulses were quite significant in the diet. In general they were dried, stored, and used after soaking, though beans, peas and chickpeas were also liked fresh. Lentils may have been the commonest of all pulses. Peas were perhaps seen less often while chickpeas served both as a staple and as a dessert, for which they were roasted or — if young and tender — eaten fresh.

While there are regions of Greece renowned for the cultivation of specific pulses, other parts of the country are known for specific bean recipes. Santorini is known for its many recipes for the humble yellow split pea, for example *fava*, and Rhodes and Sifnos are renowned for their chick pea dishes. On Sifnos, the local specialty is a slow-cooked, clay-baked chick pea soup that simmers all night in wood-burning ovens.

Bean soup (*fasolada*), an extremely nourishing and wholly vegetarian dish, is regarded by Rena Salaman, the popular author of *Greek Food*, as the national dish. Other staples are those made with lentils and chick peas. Each of these soups have their own traditional ingredients but what really makes them all particularly special is the olive oil that is usually added at the end of the cooking time.

On Crete no legume captures the local imagination among cooks as much as the ancient broad bean, which islanders savour both fresh and dried.

One of the oldest legumes are black eyed peas, and in the Peloponnese cooks have a special affinity for them. Simply boiled, they make an appetizing summer salad combined with chopped fresh onions, parsley or dill, and capers. But the one Greek legume that stands by far above all others, as an ambassador of the elegant simplicity of the best Greek cooking, and as fodder for modern chefs, is the Greek giant bean, *gigantes*. The dish *fasolia gigantes plaki* – basically beans baked in the oven with a sauce made with tomato, onion, garlic and parsley – makes one of the best vegetarian meals served in Greek homes and is customarily found as a *meze* in tavernas. The *gigantes* are native to Greece, and the ones from Kastoria are especially prized, as well as the ones from Florina and Drama regions – all three have the PGI-designation or are recognised by the EU as products of Protected Geographical Indication.

Due to the long periods of religious fasting (over 200 days a year) that prohibit most animal products, beans are the main source of protein. As a result, Greek cuisine has several bean dishes as main courses. Traditionally, Greeks would eat beans at least twice a week but it is beyond doubt that their eating habits have changed dramatically in the past 50 years. Postwar prosperity saw a rejection of many traditional foods like pulses, which had been associated with poverty. Fortunately, according to recent market surveys, the consumption of beans is again on the rise in Greece. Now more than ever, due to the financial crisis, Greeks are looking for cheap meals and beans are the superstars. Not only are they cheap, but they are rich in antioxidants and fibre, which protect one from chronic diseases such as diabetes and cancer, plus they are an excellent source of protein.

Pasta (*zimarika*)

It may be a surprise to discover that Greeks, in addition to being great eaters of bread, are also large consumers of pasta which has always been part of their larder and before refrigeration it was a necessity.

The traditional, old-fashioned dishes made with regional Greek pasta are some of the most delicious foods one finds in certain parts of the country. In the Ionian Islands a dish such as *pastitsio*, a form of lasagne, is part of their Italian heritage. Another dish favoured in particular by island communities is *youvetsi*, which derives its name from the brick red, round, terracotta dish in which it is baked. It is a hearty and delicious combination of lamb with fresh tomatoes and *kritharaki*, a rice-shaped pasta. The name means 'little barley', because it was originally made from this grain, but it is now a durum wheat semolina product. As Rena Salaman explains: "Despite the 'pasta' aspect of the dish, there are hardly any similarities to any of the Italian pasta dishes. A real *yiouvetsi* has its pasta deliciously overcooked and impregnated with the meat juices and the sweetness of the sugary fresh tomatoes."

Octopus (*htapodi*)

It is only natural in a country with so many islands and such an extensive coastline that the fruits of the sea should be an important part of the diet. Although the supply of fish in the Aegean and Mediterranean is dwindling, fish and seafood continue to be important and beloved foods to the Greeks. In the context of the Greek-Mediterranean diet, oily fish such as sardines, anchovies, and mackerels are an important part of the culinary traditions. But the most iconic of all Greek sea creatures and preparations is surely the octopus, grilled and stewed and savoured in every part of the country.

The cephalopods, so-called because their tentacles grow directly out of their heads, occur in large numbers in the Aegean, and a dish containing octopus, is always a welcome treat.

A very typical sound anywhere at the seaside is the steady slapping of octopus being tenderized as they are beaten against some suitable rock. After tenderizing the octopus is often hung up to dry before being scorched on charcoal. Greeks regard barbecued '*htapothi liasto*' (sun-dried octopus) very highly as a *meze*. But whether it is grilled, fried, stuffed, or braised in red wine, the pearly white meat is always a delicacy and is a mealtime treat at any time of the year, even during Lent.

Almonds (*amygdala*)

Per capita consumption of tree nuts in Greece is the highest in the EU and one of the highest in the world, and almonds are undoubtedly the favourite. They are an important component of the Greek diet, with the trees, like olive trees, found everywhere in the country.

Almonds appear in Greek myths and Robert Graves tells the story of Phyllis, a Thracian princess, who was in love with Acamas, a son of Theseus who had gone to fight at Troy. "When Troy fell, and the Athenian fleet returned, Phyllis paid frequent visits to the shore, hoping to sight his ship: but this had been delayed by a leak, and she died of grief after her ninth fruitless visit, at a place called Enneodos. She was metamorphosed by Athene into an almond-tree, and Acamas, arriving on the following day, embraced only her rough bark. In response to his caresses the branches burst into flower instead of leaf, which has been a peculiarity of almond-trees ever since."

Almonds feature in a variety of traditional Greek recipes. Eaten instead of meat and dairy products during religious fasts, they are also symbols of long life and happiness. No traditional wedding is complete without sugar-coated almonds (*koufeta)* being used in various ways, including an uneven number in a tulle bag being presented to each guest immediately after the ceremony. Almonds are the central ingredient in various Greek pastries, cakes, biscuits and desserts and are also used in many spoon sweets. They are also used in an almond confectionery called *amygdalota*, and similar versions are made in many places.

Walnuts (*karydia*)

The walnut was the most important nut from a health standpoint in the ancient Mediterranean world. Its medicinal virtues were detailed in many Greek and Roman medical writings. Pedanius Dioscorides (c. 40 – 90 AD), a Greek physician in the Roman army, travelled extensively and came to know many of the plants of the Mediterranean. His only surviving work, a 5-volume encyclopaedia about herbal medicine in his native Greek, was completed about the middle of the first century and widely read for more than 1500 years. He esteemed walnuts for medicinal purposes and believed that when they were eaten with the herb rue and figs they counteracted poisons. Walnuts along with honey and rue helped with "inflammation of the breasts, abscesses and dislocations." In addition to the various properties he credited the nuts with he wrote that if the kernels were burnt, ground with wine and oil, and applied to an infant's head, the child's hair would grow abundantly, and bald spots would disappear.

In one form or another walnut, the most beloved nut after the almond, is found everywhere in Greece. Since time immemorial Greeks have enjoyed the intoxicating combination of nuts and honey, especially walnuts and honey. Today that combination is still popular, and so high in calories and energy, that it is thought to be an aphrodisiac. In ancient Greece, sweetmeats that must have resembled the nut brittles of today seem to have abounded.

There is a wide variety of nut-based sweets from all over the country. In fact even the familiar baklava comes in many versions, some prepared with almonds, some with walnuts, some with pistachios, some with pine nuts, and some with combinations of these.

Nuts play a main role in another of Greece's best known pastries, *kataifi,* a kind of roll made with shredded-wheat-like pastry and doused with honey syrup. Two of the best-loved winter sweets are the delicious, spiced *karydopita,* or walnut cake, and *melo-makarona,* the traditional Christmas biscuits often either topped with walnuts or filled with them and dipped in honey syrup. Crushed walnuts also find their way onto the very popular crisp, fried dough fritters (or folds) called *diples.*

Walnuts are also an important addition to the savoury cuisine of the Greeks. Ground, they are used even more than almonds as a thickener and base for many sauces. In northern Greece ground walnuts add body and a pleasant earthy, and discreet bitterness to *melitzanosalata* (aubergine salad) and to *skordalia.* Walnuts, pine nuts, chestnuts, and almonds also all find their way into a variety of pies and stuffings in the Greek kitchen.

Pistachios *(fistikia)*

The cultivation of pistachios started on the island of Aegina around 1860 and eventually spread from there to various other parts of Greece. The pistachios from Aegina are regarded as the best in Greece and almost a quarter of the 84 square kilometres of the island are now covered by these deciduous trees that can live for a hundred years. The male and female flowers grow on separate trees, so one male tree is required for about 7 female ones that flower biennially.

Like almonds and walnuts the pistachios are generally used in pastries and desserts. Baklava and other small, honeyed *fyllo* pastries are often filled with crushed pistachios.

Honey (*meli*)

Honey was the most prestigious sweetener in ancient Greece, and although the domestication of bees *(melissa)* may have come relatively late, it was regarded as a prime food to foragers.

Honey is a traditional quality Greek product and one of the country's top exports. Greece, despite its small size, is very suitable for apiculture due to its rich flora and temperate climate, and probably has more bee hives per square kilometre than any other country in Europe. The practice and knowledge of the art of apiculture are typically passed from generation to generation. Those who practice the art are true nomads, moving their hives across the country and into the mountains looking for concentrated areas of blossoming, or forests thick with coniferous trees, to obtain honey with the purest flavour. With the richest flora in the Mediterranean basin — more than 7,500 different species of herbs, plants, wild flowers and trees — it is not surprising that the bees produce multiple types of honey. The best is that from the thyme (*thymari*) found wild in the dry, rocky Mediterranean regions. Renowned for its aroma and flavour, it is produced between the second half of June and the first half of July. The colour of thyme honey is light amber to amber when liquid, beige to brown when it is crystallized. It is a very strong, intensely aromatic honey with resinous, herbal, savoury flavours.

The fir honey from Vitina in the Peloponnese has Protected Designation of Origin. Connoisseurs say that the most mineral rich honey is pine honey and that the honey produced in the early fall, after the heather has blossomed, is also extremely beneficial. In the Greek kitchen honey is the most ancient sweetener, and it is still used as such today in a wide array of classic and contemporary confections. It also lends depth and balance to many a savoury dish, especially baked beans and some lamb and goat preparations.

Yoghurt (*yiaourti*)

Yoghurt is about as ancient as milk. It was the first and most immediate way to preserve milk by extending its life for several weeks. Stored in bags made from the linings of sheep's stomachs, the milk was subjected to both the friendly activities of the inherent bacteria and the warmth of the sun: solidified; and, because they were the correct bacteria, was preserved without turning sour.

In Greece it is only relatively recently that yoghurt has become readily available in supermarkets, pre-packaged in small cartons. In towns it was customary to buy it from the local dairy in the same way as milk or from the yogurt man as he made his rounds through one's neighbourhood.

Yogurt used to be sold in larger and smaller shallow clay pots, with the empty cleaned pots returned. The real traditional sheep's-milk yoghurt in clay containers — the kind that is rich, thick and sour, with a creamy-coloured crust (*kaimaki*) on top, and which thickens even more after a few days in the refrigerator — can still be found in small provincial towns and on some of the islands. On Crete, for example, some places are renowned for their yoghurt, so thick that it can almost be cut into slabs.

Although strained yoghurt (*yiaourti strangisto* or *sakkoulas*) was available and was known as yoghurt from the 'bag' because it was hung in fabric bags for the whey to drain off, it was regarded as 'fancier' and was more expensive. The majority of Greek yoghurt now sold in supermarkets at home and abroad is made from cow's milk and has been strained, removing up to 97% of the whey so that it takes 4 kilograms of milk to make 1 kilogram of yoghurt. Many Greeks consider the regular unstrained yoghurt made from sheep's milk healthier, and some parents prefer to give their children this traditional version. Some older Greeks feel that without the whey, the modern strained type cannot even be considered to be yoghurt.

In Greece yoghurt is served plain, usually with honey and walnuts or fruit, or mixed in sauces, salad dressings and dips. It is often served with vegetables, particularly stuffed vegetarian ones such as *dolmathes*, and is also used, together with a lot of eggs, as a filling for a savoury pie called *yiaourtopita.*

Wine (*krasí*)

Wine, together with bread and olives, has obviously been an essential staple and inherent part of the myth and culture pretty much continuously throughout the history of Greece. Dionysus, the son of Zeus and Semele a mortal, was worshipped as the god who gave man wine. The ancient Greeks honoured the god and his gift by means of feasts held on every possible occasion, and at *symposia* which were highly ritualized drinking parties for men. Scenes depicting the revelry have been immortalised as the decoration on pottery used at these functions for storing, mixing, pouring and drinking the wine.

All over Greece until fairly recently wine was something traditionally home-produced by farmers for personal consumption, and almost every household grew enough to meet all its needs. It was an activity filled with family pride, using techniques and equipment passed on from father to son. Once again this is a dwindling tradition though fortunately still alive in a few individuals.

Vines grow everywhere in abundance. They climb over pergolas and walls shading courtyards, alleys and gardens. These days the grapes are used mainly for eating and, of course, the tender fresh vine leaves are stuffed with either a vegetarian or meat filling – the delicious *dolmathes.*

In recent years the Greek wine industry has undergone enormous improvement, with serious investments in modern wine making technology. The new generation of native winemakers is being trained in the best wine schools around the world and their efforts are paying off as Greek wines continue to receive the highest awards in international competitions as well as the recognition they deserve throughout the world.

What makes Greek wine so unique are the more than 300 indigenous grape varieties grown there, some of which have been cultivated since ancient times. Many of the world's leading wine critics agree that the distinct flavours that come from these native grape varieties are a strong marketing advantage for the Greek wine industry.

Metaxa

Metaxa, brandy-like spirit, was founded in 1888 by Spiros Metaxa, the descendant of a family of silk merchants, who dreamed of creating a spirit that would attain an entirely new degree of taste, smoothness and refinement. It is still produced using the method he developed. The raw materials are wines made from sun-dried Savatiano, Sultanina and Korinthiaki varieties of grape. From these a brandy of 82 – 86% volume is distilled in two processes which do justice to the different characters of the wines. This basic brandy matures for a number of years in barrels of Limousin oak.

This first process already produces the delicate taste so characteristic of Metaxa, and its amber colour. Before the next stage it is passed through a secret bouquet of selected Mediterranean herbs and fragrant May rose petals that have macerated for a full year with distillates. Then the distillation is blended, or married, with mature Muscat wine from the islands of Lemnos and Samos, and finally matured again in oak barrels until it has fully developed its unmistakable bouquet and achieved the desired quality.

There are four main grades of Metaxa - indicated by 3, 5, 7 and 12 stars - containing progressively older distillate and different proportions of the main ingredients. The 3- and 5-star versions are fruit-flavoured and light in body, while the 7 and 12 stars are more flavoursome and complex. Older blends are available, some containing distillates aged for up to 30 years, but they are rarely found outside of Greece.

Ouzo

No other beverage is as closely associated with Greece as this clear, anise-flavoured spirit and every region of the country produces its own version. It can be drunk either neat or, as is most common, mixed with iced water when it turns a milky opaque colour. If ice is added directly to the ouzo it creates unsightly crystals on the surface of the drink. It is traditionally consumed as an aperitif, or as an after-dinner drink, at celebrations, and as an after-work pick-me-up. It is an ideal accompaniment to *mezes*, the traditional small plates of Greek appetizers.

With a distinct licorice flavour, ouzo is generally based on pure alcohol from various sources. For example, it could be a distillation of molasses produced during sugar manufacture. The alcohol is diluted with water and is then flavoured with aniseed, and sometimes other aromatic herbs such as fennel, star anise, coriander, cardamom, angelica, lime flowers and others. On the North Aegean island of Lesvos, which has the oldest tradition of ouzo production, a trace of mastic (see page) may also be part of the recipe. This mixture is left to stand overnight so that the herbs can release their flavours and the next day is distilled several times in large copper vats.

Isolating the 'middle run', the heart (*kardia*), is the true art of the distiller, as both the forerun or head (*kefali*) and after run or tail (*oura*) contain elements affecting the taste. The heart is then distilled slowly a second and sometimes even a third time under constant supervision. The *adoloto,* the middle portion of the last distillation is then stored for several months in large stainless steel tanks to ripen and ensure that homogeneity of the mixture is achieved. Before bottling it is finally adjusted to the correct grade of alcohol - usually about 37.5 to 45% - using crystal-clear or distilled water.

In Greece today even the smallest villages have an *ouzeria* (ouzo bar), similar to the French wine bar, that specialize in many different types of ouzo that are always served with something from their tantalizing array of *mezethes.* These are convivial gathering places for men and women, and patrons typically linger over their drinks and food.

Ouzo is also used in cooking to add a distinct anise flavour to various dishes from seafood marinades to cakes, ice cream and spoon sweets. Some believe that ouzo — or more specifically anise — has healing properties and will use it to ease an upset stomach or relieve a headache. Parents of teething babies will often rub a bit of ouzo on their infant's gums to soothe their discomfort.

Mezethes

A *meze*, or *mezethaki* (the addition of the suffix *-aki* suggests the diminutive form of things) is usually translated as 'appetizer,' and many of the little dishes are served with ouzo or wine in homes, tavernas, *kafenion* and *ouzeri.* They can be served as hors d'oeuvres or as first courses, but the translation hardly does justice to the sheer range, ingenuity, and pleasure of *mezethes*, nor to their fundamental place in Greek tradition. A *meze* in Greece is always offered with a drink, as Greeks never drink without eating at the same time. Simple ones found everywhere are plates of olives and feta cheese. This civilized custom has been an integral part of the fabric of Greek life since antiquity. The doctors and scholars of that time knew that drinking wine on an empty stomach was not a good idea so, with characteristic creative logic, they made it impossible for Greek society to indulge in such a barbaric practice, and tasty little plates of food became available whenever drinks were served.

Other typical *mezes* include crispy fried rings of *kalamarakia* (squid), *tzatziki* (yogurt, cucumber and garlic dip), *taramosalata* (fish-roe pate), *dolmathes* (stuffed vine leaves), small *tyropitta* (cheese pies), and *keftethes* (small round meatballs) to name but a few.

Mezethes vary according to season and location and reflect the country's colourful history. The skill of composing a successful *meze* table lies in the balance of ingredients, and the essence of the experience is the surprise and pleasure of sampling a variety of intense contrasting flavours and textures in small mouthfuls.

Meatballs *(keftedes)*

Note: Daphne says that the secret of tasty meatballs is adding mint and lots of onions. The Lesvian characteristic is the cumin and, of course, the ouzo! She adds that the mixture must be soft but should not stick to one's hands.

***Ingredients** (serves 5-6)*

1 kg beef mince
250 g bread minus crusts
1 egg
2 big onions
2 handfuls of mint
2 handfuls of parsley
1 tbsp vinegar
½ cup of ouzo
½ cup of olive oil
1 tsp cumin
Salt/black pepper freshly ground
Flour for dusting
Oil for frying (sunflower)

1 Put mince into a deep bowl.

2 Soak bread in water and then squeeze out the water very well.

3 Finely chop the onions, the mint and the parsley.

4 Add all the ingredients to the mince, mixing it well by hand, and then leave in the fridge for about 30 minutes for the flavours to blend.

5 Heat the oil for frying in a pan and, while this is happening, take small amounts of the mixture forming them into small squashed balls and dust them with flour shaking off the excess before frying.

6 Fry in the hot oil for a short time on both sides, turning with a spoon so as not to break them. After frying remove excess oil with absorbent paper.

Potato balls *(patatokeftedes)*

Ingredients (for about 30+ balls)

1 kg potatoes
1 cup of medium-hard yellow cheese grated
2 eggs
½ a bunch of parsley
1 tsp nutmeg
1 tsp cumin
Breadcrumbs (optional)
Salt/pepper
Oil for frying (sunflower)
Flour for dusting

1 Peel, boil and then mash the potatoes.

2 Finely chop the parsley.

3 Add to the potatoes the eggs, cheese, parsley and cumin, mix well, and season with salt and pepper.

4 If the mixture is not sufficiently dry add some breadcrumbs.

5 Heat the oil in a frying pan and, while this is happening, roll a small amount of the mixture with dampened hands into a ball (about the size of a table tennis ball), flattened slightly. Dust them with flour shaking off the excess before frying.

6 Fry in the hot oil for a short time on both sides, turning with a spoon so as not to break them. After frying remove excess oil with absorbent paper.

Note: As an alternative the balls can be dredged in egg and bread crumbs before being fried.
All these different balls called various things in English – rissoles, fritters and croquettes – are very popular among Greeks and make excellent *mezes.* Every Greek cook has a favourite recipe, and method, for preparing them and some like to make them completely round as below.

Carrot balls *(karotokeftedes)*

Note: The follow ingredients are sufficient for approximately 30 balls.

Ingredients

4 cups of grated carrot
2 cups of chopped onion
2 cups of finely chopped celery
4 cups of finely chopped spinach
2 cups of finely chopped green pepper
½ cup of olive oil

For the batter:
3 eggs
3-4 tbsp flour
3-4 tbsp breadcrumbs
A little milk
Salt/black pepper freshly ground
Oil for frying (sunflower)

For garnishing:
Greek yogurt
2 tomatoes finely chopped
A few basil leaves

1 Grate the carrots and chop the onions, celery, pepper and spinach.

2 Heat the olive oil in a frying pan and lightly fry the onion, carrot, celery and pepper until they have softened.

3 Add the spinach and cook until all the liquid has been absorbed.

4 In a large bowl mix the eggs, flour, breadcrumbs and milk. To this add the vegetable mixture, season with salt and pepper and mix well. If the mixture is too liquid add more breadcrumbs to thicken.

5 Heat the oil and in the very hot oil fry spoonfuls of the mixture. When both sides are sufficiently done remove and dry on absorbent paper.

6 Serve the flat 'balls' with a garnish on top of one teaspoon of yogurt, some finely chopped tomato and a sprinkle of basil.

Note: Daphne explains that using the same main ingredients one can make more traditional and less sophisticated carrot balls as follows:

1 Grate the carrots and finely chop the onion, celery, pepper and spinach. Put these ingredients into a bowl and add the eggs, season with salt and pepper.

2 Hand-mix it all well adding some breadcrumbs till the mixture is not liquid.

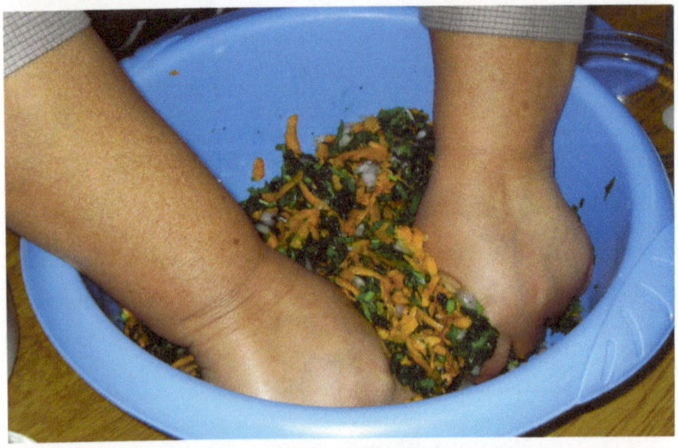

3 Heat the oil in a frying pan and, while this is happening, roll a small amount of the mixture with dampen hands into a ball (about the size of a table tennis ball). Dust them with flour shaking off the excess before frying.

4 Fry in the hot oil for a short time on both sides turning with a spoon so as not to break them. After frying remove excess oil with absorbent paper.

Note: There is a traditional Lesvian recipe for fried onion and fennel balls as follows:

Toss together crumbled feta (about 500g) with grated medium-hard yellow cheese (about 125g) and add a bunch of fennel finely chopped and a bunch of spring onions also finely chopped. To this add 5 beaten eggs and season with pepper - no need to add salt because the cheese is salty enough. Gradually add enough flour to turn the mixture into a very thick batter almost like a soft dough.

Heat olive oil in a deep pan and drop into it spoonfuls of the batter. When the fried balls rise to the surface and are browned all over, remove them with a slotted spoon and put them onto absorbent paper towels, which may need to be changed a couple of times, so that the excess oil is absorbed.

Zucchini balls *(kolokithokeftedes)*

Ingredients (for about 12 balls)

4 medium sized zucchini (courgettes)
1 cup breadcrumbs
1 large onion
½ cup of medium- hard yellow cheese grated
½ a bunch of dill
½ a bunch of parsley
1 handful of chopped mint (fresh or dry)
2 eggs
Salt/black pepper freshly ground
Oil for frying (sunflower)
Flour for dusting

1 Wash and then coarsely grate the zucchini.

2 Add salt to the grated zucchini and allow it to stand for a while in a colander.

3 Remove as much fluid as possible by squeezing the grated zucchini by hand, and then put it into a bowl.

4 Finely chop the onion, dill, parsley and mint and add it all to the bowl together with eggs, cheese, breadcrumbs mixing well and season with salt and pepper.

5 Heat the oil in a frying pan and, while this is happening, roll a small amount of

the mixture with dampened (or lightly oiled) hands into a ball (about the size of a table tennis ball). Dust them with flour shaking off the excess before frying.

Note: *Domatokeftedes* is a speciality on the island of Santorini mainly because the local tomatoes are so good.
About 450 g of tomatoes are cut up together with 2 peeled and finely chopped onions. Add to this about a cup of finely chopped fresh mint, and 2 tbsps of finely chopped parsley. This is all mixed together with a tbsp of olive oil and seasoned with salt, freshly ground pepper and a little paprika. Add self-raising flour (about 150 g) gradually to make a thickish but moist paste.
Heat some sunflower oil in a frying pan and drop in spoonfuls of the mixture. Fry, turning them over until nicely golden all over. Serve immediately.

Garlic bread *(skordopsomo)*

Ingredients

1 loaf of bread
125 g soft butter
1 tsp salt
½ tsp freshly ground black pepper
2-3 garlic cloves
1 tsp finely chopped parsley
1 tsp oregano
1 tbsp finely chopped onion (optional)

1 Cut bread into slices without cutting right through the loaf.

2 Mix the butter with all the other ingredients and spread into all the cuts and over the whole of the crust.

3 Wrap the loaf in aluminium foil and bake in medium oven for 30 minutes approximately.

4 Remove foil and cut slices through.

5 Serve immediately.

Aubergine salad *(melitzanosalat)*

Ingredients

3 large aubergines
½ - ¾ cup of olive oil
Juice of ½ a lemon
1-2 garlic cloves
½ medium onion
2-3 tbsp finely chopped parsley
1 medium tomato
Salt/freshly ground black pepper

1 Wash the aubergines and then pierce 2 of them with a fork and bake in the oven until soft (180°C for 45-50 mins).

2 Using a fork if necessary, hold the third aubergine (unpierced) over an open flame until the skins are well scorched and the flesh is very soft. This will give the salad the essential smoky flavour. Set all aside to cool.

3 Crush the garlic. Deseed the tomato and dice, and finely chop the onion.

4 As soon as the aubergines can be handled cut them in half and scrape out the flesh using a spoon. Remove the big seeds if there are too many. Leave the flesh in a colander for a while to drain and then mash with a fork.

5 In a bowl mix the aubergine pulp, oil and lemon juice with a wooden spoon, stir in the garlic, onion, tomato and parsley. Season with salt and pepper.

Stuffed mushrooms *(manitaria gemista)*

Note: Sometimes Daphne does not use tomato and instead of feta uses a mild yellow cheese grated or cream cheese. In this case she flavours with nutmeg rather than with mint.

Ingredients

10 large white mushrooms
3 spring onions
1 cup parsley finely chopped
½ cup mint finely chopped (optional)
1 large zucchini
1 large tomato
100 g feta or cream cheese
2 tbsp olive oil or butter
Garlic granules or crushed fresh garlic
Salt/freshly ground black pepper

1 Wash the mushrooms, remove the stalks and chop them finely.

2 Finely chop the parsley and the spring onions including their green stems.

3 Chop up finely the tomato and the zucchini and mash the feta with a fork.

4 In a frying pan put oil or butter and heat. Add mushroom stalks, zucchini and spring onions. Cook until all the liquid is absorbed.

5 Add the tomato, salt, pepper, mint, parsley and garlic granules (to taste).

6 Take off the heat, add the feta and mix well.

7 Place the mushrooms in an oven dish and fill with the mixture. Bake in an oven at 180°C until the liquid has been absorbed and the tops are golden brown.

Zucchini (courgette) flowers stuffed with cheese *(louloudia)*

Ingredients

20 (approx.) very fresh flowers
350-400 g grated cheese (yellow cheese and feta)
1 egg
½ cup mint
Freshly ground black pepper
Oil for frying

For the batter:
1 can very cold soda water
flour (enough to make a thin batter)
a little salt

1 check the flowers and remove any insects that may be in them. Rinse them very gently under running water, then drain them.

2 Finely chop the mint.

3 In a bowl mix the cheese and egg, then add the mint and pepper.

4 Using a teaspoon carefully fill the flowers with the cheese mixture leaving room so that the leaves can be folded inward to seal them.

5 In another bowl mix the cold soda water with the flour and salt to make the batter.

6 Heat the oil, ideally in a deep pan. Dip the flowers one by one in the batter and fry until golden.

7 When fried, remove and place them on a paper kitchen towel to absorb the excess oil.

Note: One can use a tempura batter - there are various versions. One is as follows: sift the flour and salt together into a large bowl, whisk in an egg yolk and very cold soda water. An alternative: chill water in a freezer until very cold. Break an egg into a bowl and whisk in the water. Add the flour and mix very gently making sure not to make the batter smooth and leaving lumps. In other versions self-raising flour is used, an in another plain flour is combined with corn flour and sometimes a small amount of bicarbonate soda.

Tzatziki

Ingredients

500g Greek yogurt
1 cucumber
2 garlic cloves
1 tbsp vinegar
2 tbsp olive oil
1-2 tbsp dill finely chopped
Salt

1 Peel the cucumber, grate coarsely and set aside in a colander to drain.

2 Dry the cucumber by squeezing it between paper towels.

3 Combine the cucumber, yogurt, crushed garlic, vinegar, olive oil and dill in a large bowl.

4 Cover and refrigerate for at least 30 minutes, so that all the flavours are well blended

Note: Tzatziki is usually just served with bread as a *meze* but makes a very good accompaniment to crispy fried slices of zucchini or aubergine as an alternative to garlic paste (*skorthalia)* — see page 149 — and to most roast or grilled food.

Fish roe pate *(taramosalata)*

Note: One can find *tarama* (fish roe) in Greek grocery stores. The Greek *taramosalata* is usually pink because red *tarama* is used but the red is an artificial colour so it is healthier to use white *tarama.* John West has 100g tins of soft cods roe from Iceland.

Ingredients

50 g white tarama (fish roe)
½ small onion
8 slices white bread
½ cup lemon juice
1 cup olive or sunflower oil

1 Peel the onion.

2 Soak bread in water for 10 minutes then squeeze most of the water out.

3 Put all the ingredients – except for the oil – and in a blender till all are well mixed.

4 Add the oil gradually during the blending process.

5 The *taramosalata* is ready. Put it into a bowl and store in the fridge.

Split pea purée *(fava)*

Note: This is made from yellow split peas called *fava* in Greece (not to be confused with fava the bean). The peas used there are smaller, sweeter in taste and not as solid in texture when cooked than ordinary yellow peas. They are light yellow in colour and the *fava* from Santorini is highly regarded. If these are not available ordinary split peas can be used.

Ingredients

500g split peas
2 medium sized onions
1 cup olive oil
1 lemon
Salt/freshly ground black pepper
1 tsp oregano (optional)

1 *Soak the split peas in cold water for about 30 minutes and then rinse in several changes of water.*

2 *Pour 8 cups of water into a saucepan and add the split peas as well as one onion cut into 4 and ½ cup of oil; season with a little salt.*

3 *Allow the split peas to cook on a low heat until they become mushy (do not cover the pan because it will boil over).*

4 *Towards the end stir continuously with a wooden spoon so that the fava does not stick but becomes a purée. It can be purée in a food processor.*

5 *Squeeze half a lemon and cut the other half into thin slices. Cut the second onion into slices.*

6 *The purée may appear quite liquid, but as it cools down it becomes more solid.*

7 *Put the fava onto a dish and pour the lemon juice over it; season with a little pepper and salt if needed. Pour over the remaining oil. It can also be sprinkled with oregano.*

8 *Garnish the fava with the sliced lemon, onions and black olives (or capers as in the picture below).*

Zucchini crisps

Notes:
– An alternative version of fried zucchini (an aubergine) is given in Appendix 1.
– Daphne believes the crisps are tastier when eaten at room temperature and should be allowed to stand for one or two hours so that the flavour of the herbs and garlic are fully absorbed.

Ingredients

5-6 medium sized zucchini
1-2 tbsp vinegar (depending on taste)
1 handful mint
½ handful basil (dry or fresh)
3-4 garlic cloves
Salt
Oil for frying

1 Wash and cut the zucchini into thin slices.

2 In a frying pan heat the oil. When the oil is hot fry the thinly sliced zucchini.

3 When light brown on both sides remove with a slotted spoon and place on paper towel to absorb excess oil.

5 Finely chop the mint and basil.

6 Finely chop or press the garlic

7 When the zucchini crisps have dried out place them in a deep bowl, add salt and then the mint, basil and garlic.

8 Sprinkle with vinegar and mix well.

Spinach rolls

Ingredients

500 g fyllo pastry
1 kg spinach
4-5 eggs
½-¾ kg feta cheese
3-4 medium size onions
1 bunch dill
4-5 spring onions
1 cup olive oil
Salt/freshly ground black pepper

1 Finely chop the onions, cut the spring onions into thin pieces, cut the dill finely and chop the spinach coarsely.

2 In a pan heat most of the oil and sauté the onions. Then add the spring onions, dill and spinach. Stir until all the liquid has evaporated.

3 Take off the heat, add the feta cheese cut into small pieces and the eggs. Season with salt (taking care because the cheese has salt in it) and pepper mixing it all well.

4 Lay out the fyllo and with a sharp knife cut it into strips about 15-20cm wide (ie divide the long side into 3), making sure to cut through all layers.

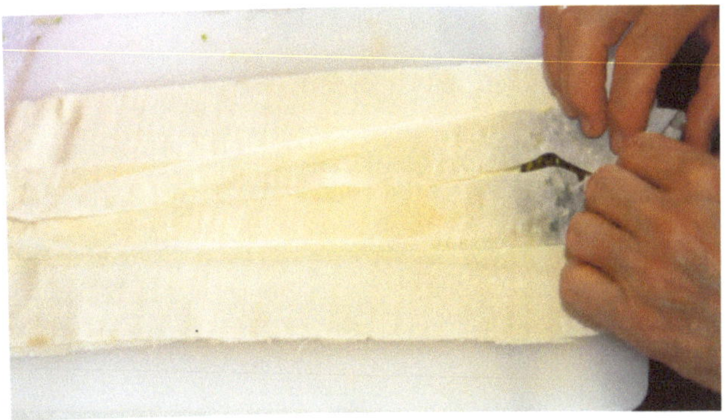

5 Brush a strip of the fyllo with oil and put a teaspoon of the mixture in the centre near the end. Fold in the two sides and then roll up the fyllo tightly.

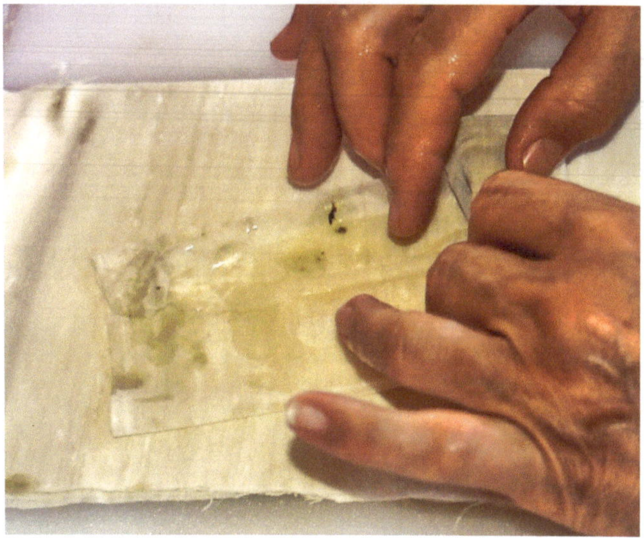

6 Put the roll into an oven dish which has been brushed with oil.

7 Repeat steps 5 and 6 with the rest of the fyllo leaving a little space between each roll in the oven dish. When all the rolls are in the dish brush their tops with oil again.

8 Bake in a hot oven (about 190°C) until golden brown. Remove from the oven and let stand for a few minutes.

Stuffed peppers with feta
(piperies gemistes me feta)

Note: There are many varieties of peppers, and they often have different names depending on region. The peppers used for this recipe are a long horn-shaped mild or sweet type.

Ingredients

10 green peppers
100 g feta cheese
1 tomato
1 onion
½ bunch parsley
1 red pepper (not hot)
4 tbsp olive oil
Freshly ground black pepper

1 Wash the peppers, cut off the tops and put these to the side. Take out the seeds.

2 Cut the tomato and red pepper into small cubes, then finely chop the onion and parsley.

3 Crumble the feta and mix all the ingredients well.

4 Fill the peppers with the mixture.

5 Brush an oven dish with oil and place the peppers in it next to each other. Close them with their tops.

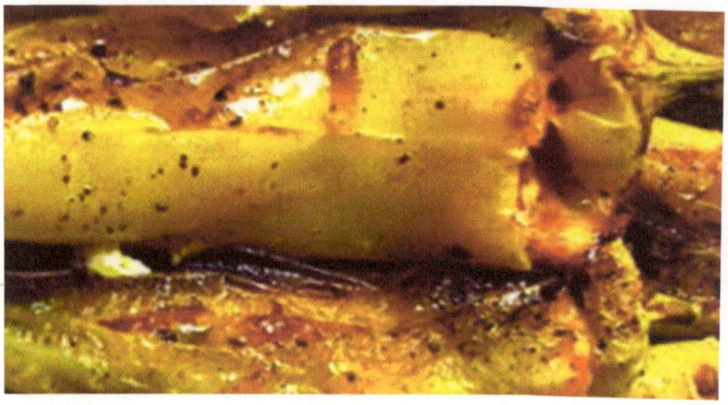

6 Spread the rest of the oil on top of the peppers.

7 Bake in the oven at 170°C for about 30 minutes.

Note: Daphne says that while she likes the theory, she has never succeeded in sealing the tops well – there is always some filling spilling out. But this does not concern her any longer because she has discovered that she enjoys the 'out-side' baked filling better than the 'inside'!

Omelette with tomato
(strapatsada)

Notes:
– In most regions of Greece this popular traditional summer dish — when tomatoes abound — is known as *kagianas*. In the Ionian islands it is called *strapatsada* from the Italian verb *strapazzare*, which means to handle roughly (to beat). Due to the availability and low cost of its basic ingredients (fresh tomatoes, eggs and olive oil) as well as being quick and easy to prepare it is often served for lunch or a light snack; however, it can also be eaten cold. As one can imagine, there are many different variations with many possible add-ins, and Daphne's version is as below.
– Although a simple dish, with the right fresh, juicy, flavoursome tomatoes it can be a very appetizing and delicious.

Ingredients

5-6 eggs
2-3 ripe tomatoes
2 peppers
2-3 spring onions
½ bunch parsley
100 g feta cheese
1 cup medium hard yellow cheese
4 tbsp olive oil
½ tsp oregano
Salt/freshly ground black pepper

1 Finely chop the spring onions and their green stalks, the onion, peppers, tomatoes and parsley.

2 Crumble the feta or mash with a fork.

3 Heat oil in a frying pan and lightly fry spring onions, onions and peppers until soft.

4 Add the tomatoes and lower the heat. Cook until the sauce has thickened.

5 Break the eggs one at a time and mix in with a wooden spoon.

6 When the eggs and the ingredients have blended add parsley, cheese, salt, pepper and oregano, mix well till eggs are cooked. The consistency should resemble scrambled eggs. Serve with fresh bread or toast.

Baked feta *(feta psiti)*

Note: An easy appetizer that never fails to impress! People are familiar with feta, but this traditional Greek way of preparing it is not as well known. The salty/sour taste of the feta offsets the heat of the chili flakes - so don't be afraid to use them. The tomato also really adds a certain freshness to the density of the cheese. Serve with bread to soak up all the delicious juices that collect at the bottom of the foil. Another way to enjoy this baked feta is to turn it into a dip. Wait for 2-3 minutes for it to cool a little and then put it into a food processor.

Ingredients *(for one person)*

1 piece of feta cheese 2cm thick
1 slice of tomato
1 ring of green pepper
2 tsp olive oil
Oregano
Freshly ground black pepper
Cayenne pepper (optional)
Chilli flakes (optional)

1 Put the feta onto a piece of aluminium foil big enough to enclose the cheese fully.

2 Put the slice of tomato and the pepper ring on top of the feta.

3 Sprinkle with olive oil, oregano, pepper as well as the cayenne and/or chilli flakes if they are used.

4 Enclose it all tightly in the foil and put this into a baking dish.

5 Bake in a medium hot oven for 20 minutes.

Cheese pie *(tyropita)*

Notes:
– Daphne say that if one wishes one can use only feta cheese just as they used to do when she was young.
– See also the note for spinach pie on page 56.

Ingredients

500 g fyllo pastry
2 tbsp plain flour
2 tbsp butter
3 cups milk
2 eggs
250 g feta cheese
150 g gouda cheese
100 g graviera (or other medium hard cheese)
½-1 tsp ground nutmeg, or oregano
½ cup olive oil
Salt/freshly ground black pepper

1 Melt the butter in a small pan, add the flour and stir continuously till it takes on a light brown colour.

2 Gradually add the milk stirring with a whisk; when thickened take off the heat and leave to cool (béchamel).

3 To the béchamel add the cheese, nutmeg, salt, pepper and eggs. Mix well.

4 Oil an oven dish and in it layer four sheets of *fyllo* pastry. Use a soft pastry brush to lightly coat each sheet separately with olive oil. Start at the edges (to keep them from cracking) and work in toward the centre. Spread the filling evenly over the *fyllo* with a spoon.

5 Layer 4-5 *fyllo* sheets on top of the filling, brushing oil onto each sheet separately as before.

6 Seal the edges of the pie by twisting the *fyllo* towards the dish. (Some people suggest using water or a beaten egg to seal the top layer of *fyllo* to the bottom layer).

7 Score the uncooked pie into diamond or square shapes with a sharp knife. Be careful not to cut through more than the top couple of layers because if the cuts are too deep the filling will spill out. Bake at 160°C for about 40 minutes, then increase the temperature to 180°C and continue to bake for another 15 minutes until the pie is golden brown.

Note: Tissue-thin sheets of *fyllo* pastry can be frustrating to work with because they can dry out quickly and tear. They thaw more evenly and are less likely to stick together if left unopened in the fridge overnight. Do not open until all the other ingredients have been prepared and one is ready to work. Unroll the *fyllo* sheets and lay them flat on a dry surface. Immediately cover with plastic wrap and then a damp towel. (Covering with just a damp towel will moisten the sheets and make them stick together.) Keep the *fyllo* covered when not working with it, and don't leave it uncovered for too long. Work as fast as possible.

Small cheese pies *(tyropitakia)*

Note: These little individual cheese pies are the quintessential Greek savoury snack food and a great favourite.

Ingredients

For the dough:
500 g self-raising flour
150 g yoghurt
250 g butter (at room temperature)
1 egg
Salt/freshly ground black pepper

For the filling:
1 cup yellow cheese grated
½ cup feta cheese crumbled/mashed
1 egg
½ cup mint
¼ cup fresh cream (optional)
Freshly ground black pepper

1 Put the flour into a deep bowl with salt and pepper. Add the butter and rub it in.

2 Add yoghurt and mix. Add a few drops of warm water or a little flour, if necessary, so that the dough is malleable.

3 Leave to rest and prepare filling.

4 Beat the eggs in a deep bowl.

5 Add the yellow cheese, feta, mint, cream and pepper and mix it all well.

6 Take a table-tennis -size ball of dough and flatten it on a floured board.

7 Put half a teaspoon of the filling in the middle and fold into a half-moon shape. Press the edges together decoratively with finger or spoon so that the filling does not spill out.

8 Place the *tyropitakia* in a baking dish. These pies swell when baked, so leave space between them otherwise they will stick together.

9 Brush some egg or milk onto the tops to get a better colour when baked.

10 Bake in a preheated oven at 180°C for 20 minutes until golden brown.

Note: When these small, individual pies are made with homemade pastry of various sorts they are usually of a half-moon shape. They can of course easily be made using *fyllo* pastry but then their shape is usually that of a small triangle (*trigona* in Greek).

Desperate housewife's cheese pie

Ingredients

4-5 handfuls of plain flour
2 eggs
250 g feta cheese
100 g butter
About ½ cup water
Oregano
½ tsp salt
Freshly ground black pepper

1 Put flour, eggs and salt into a bowl and mix well.

2 Add water gradually while stirring to get a light batter.

3 Brush an oven dish well with butter and pour in the batter.

4 Crumble the *feta* and sprinkle it over the batter as well as the oregano and pepper. Add some blobs of butter to the top of the batter.

5 Bake in a preheated oven at 180°C for about 15 minutes. Don't overbake the pie — when the edges are brown it is ready.

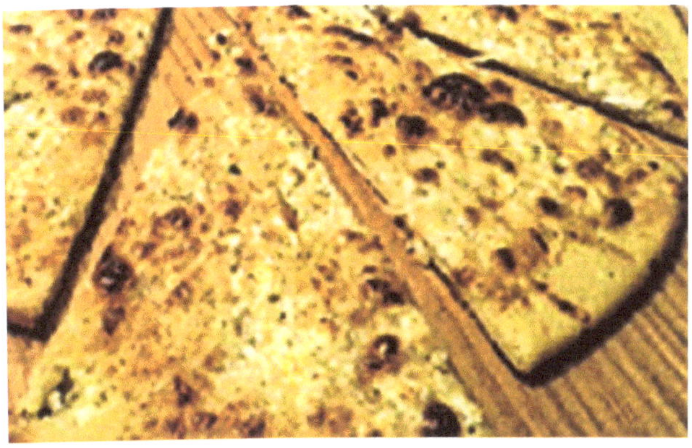

Vegetable dishes

The Greek diet has been essentially a vegetarian one for eons. As ingredients in stews and soup, and as relishes eaten fresh with bread and olive oil and cheese, green and root vegetables have been essentials in the Greek diet since earliest historical times; in poorer households and simpler circumstances they have been all the more important, taking the place of unattainable meat and fish.

Contemporary Greeks generally eat meals created almost entirely from plant foods. As a result their menu of vegetable dishes is a wonder: single vegetable dishes accented by olive oil, lemon, herbs, cheese or savoury sauces; vegetable stews in which a splurge of vegetables is braised to form a complex medley; baked vegetables; vegetables mixed with flour, onions and herbs and fried into crisp croquettes and fritters, or turned into tarts. Lastly, every vegetable and leaf that can serve as a container is stuffed.

Because vegetables are often the main dish at a meal, not just a side show, they have to be excellent. Over centuries of fasting, whether prescribed by the Church or by necessity, Greeks have perfected techniques of combining simple ingredients to make them taste good and go further, to feed large families. In this they have been amply assisted by nutritious, delicious olive oil which is required by virtually every vegetable dish.

Baked vegetables (tourlou)

Ingredients

4 potatoes
1-2 zucchini
1-2 aubergines
1 yellow pepper
1 red pepper (not chilli)
2 large onions
1-2 carrots
1½ tins (400 + 200g) chopped tomatoes
1-2 tsp sugar
1 bunch of parsley
¾ cup olive oil
1 handful of oregano or mint
Salt/ freshly ground black pepper

1 Peel, wash, and cut the potatoes and carrots into medium sized pieces.

2 Wash the aubergines and zucchini and cut into medium thick slices. Wash the pepper, cut into large pieces removing the seeds.

3 Peel and cut the onions into large slices. Wash and finely chop the parsley.

4 Place all these ingredients into an oven dish.

5 Add the rest of the ingredients: chopped tomatoes, sugar, oil, oregano and salt and pepper. Mix it all well. Daphne adds the sugar to cut the sourness of the tomatoes.

6 Bake in oven at 180°C for about an hour and 15 minutes.

7 After 45 minutes take out of the oven, stir all with a wooden spoon and check, then add liquid to ensure that it does not dry out.

8 At the end of the baking time check to see if the *tourlou* is ready by testing the potatoes with a fork. Normally there is no liquid but just a little thick sauce.

Baked giant beans *(gigantes)*

Note: Daphne says that this recipe seems easy but it took her two or three times to cook it correctly. Her problem was that it dried up and there was no sauce left. Now she always uses a whole cup of olive oil. One can use fresh ripe tomatoes skinned and diced rather than the canned ones. It is important to boil the beans first.

Ingredients *(serves 2-3)*

250g butter beans
1 large onion
1-2 carrots
1 tin (400g) of chopped tomatoes
one third cup of olive oil
½ bunch of parsley
some celery (optional)
1 tsp oregano
Salt/freshly ground black pepper

1 Put beans into a large saucepan cover with water and leave to soak overnight.

2 Drain and rinse them in a colander, return them to the saucepan, cover them with plenty of cold water and boil for a short time.

3 Pour off the water and refill the pan with hot water to about 25cm over the beans. Boil until they are cooked but still a little al dente. Be very careful not to overcook them because they get mushy and then are not at their best. Drain through a colander and set aside in an ovenproof dish with lid.

4 Roughly chop the onions Cut up the parsley and celery. Peel, wash and cut the carrots into slices. Add these to the beans together with the tomato, oregano, salt, pepper and oil.

5 Mix all the ingredients well and add 1 or 2 cups of water. Bake in the oven at 200°C for about 1½ hours. Check during this time whether it is necessary to add more water. The dish is ready when the beans have softened, and the sauce has thickened. Be careful not to let it all dry out.

Stuffed tomatoes and peppers *(gemista)*

Note: Daphne says that sometimes she doesn't fry the onions, garlic, tomato pulp and rice but just makes the mixture in a bowl and fills the tomatoes and peppers with this. It is easier and the result is just as good.

Ingredients (serves 6 as a starter; 3 or 4 as a main course)
6 tomatoes (tennis ball size)
6 peppers (tennis ball size)
12 handfuls of risotto rice
1 bunch parsley finely chopped
1 handful mint
1 handful oregano
1-2 handfuls of grated parmesan cheese
1 cup olive oil
2 large onions thickly grated
2 garlic cloves crushed (optional)
1 tsp sugar
Salt/freshly ground black pepper

1 Wash the tomatoes and peppers. Cut thin round slices off their tops and put aside.

2 Scoop out the tomato pulp with a spoon and place in a bowl. Be careful not to make a hole in the tomatoes. Scoop out the seeds of the peppers.

3 In a large frying pan add half of the oil and lightly fry the onions and garlic until they turn golden brown.

4 Add the finely shredded tomato pulp, salt, pepper, sugar and rice. Bring to the boil for a few minutes stirring continuously.

5 Remove from the heat, add the parsley, mint, oregano and cheese and mix well.

6 Pack the peppers and tomatoes tightly in an oven dish and fill them with the mixture. Do not fill to the top, leaving room for the rice to expand. To provide support one can place thick slices of potato (salted, oiled and sprinkled with oregano) in between.

7 Put the tops onto the tomatoes and peppers. Pour 1 cup of water into the dish and the remaining oil over the vegetables.

8 Bake in the oven at 180°C for about 2½ hours. Check once or twice to see if more water is needed. The dish is ready when there is only a little liquid left, mostly oil; the tomatoes and peppers have shrunk and their tops are almost black.

Aubergines Imam *(Imam)*

Ingredients (serves 4-6)

5-6 big aubergines
2-3 large onions
3-4 garlic cloves
1 bunch parsley
1½ tins (400+200g) of chopped tomatoes (or tomato passata)
1 tsp sugar
½ cup olive oil for frying
Salt/freshly ground black pepper

1 Wash the aubergines and peel in stripes (zebra-style).

2 Set the aubergines on a wooden board and make 3 deep length-wise slits in each being careful not to cut right through. Fry them on both sides till softened.

3 Cut the onions into thin slices. Finely chop the parsley and garlic.

4 Put the onion into a pan with olive oil and fry lightly. Add the tomato, parsley, garlic, salt, pepper and sugar. Mix well and cook until the sauce has thickened.

5 In a baking dish arrange the fried aubergines next to each other with the slits facing upward. Fill each slit with the tomato mixture.

6 Add a cup of water to the remaining sauce and spread over the aubergines.

7 Bake the aubergines in the oven at 180°C for about 45 minutes.

Zucchini tart *(sfougato)*

Note: the word *sfougato* comes from the Greek word '*sfougari*' meaning sponge, referring to the holes formed in the tart when the egg mixture is cooked.

Ingredients *(serves 4-5)*

3-4 zucchini, medium sized
8-10 fresh spring onions including green stems
1 bunch of dill finely chopped
2 tbsp of mint leaves finely chopped
200g feta cheese crumbled
100g medium hard cheese grated
4-5 eggs
1 cup breadcrumbs
½ cup olive oil
Salt/freshly ground pepper

1 Wash and coarsely grate the zucchini. Salt it and allow to stand in a colander for a while.

2 Squeeze and strain the zucchini taking out as much water as possible, and put into a large bowl, add the onions, dill and mint and mix well.

3 Add grated cheese, crumbled feta, eggs and breadcrumbs. Breadcrumbs are always used to help soak up the water that remains in the zucchini even if it is well strained. Add pepper, oil and salt if needed — the cheese may make it salty enough. Mix well.

4 Place mixture in an oven-proof dish which has been lightly oiled and spread it evenly in the dish.

5 Bake in oven at 180°C for about 35-40 minutes.

6 The *sfougato* is ready when the top becomes a golden brown and a knife remains dry after testing.

Leeks in egg-lemon sauce *(prassa avgalemono)*

Ingredients *(serves 4)*

2-3 leeks
1-2 carrots
1-2 potatoes
¼ cup of olive oil
¼ cup chopped dill
Salt/freshly ground black pepper

For the egg-lemon sauce:
1 egg
1 lemon
1 tbsp cornflower
Salt/freshly ground black pepper

1 Peel and wash carrots and potatoes and cut into pieces.

2 Wash and cut leeks into medium-sized pieces (both white and green parts).

3 In a deep pan heat oil and fry the leeks, carrots and potatoes lightly.

4 Add dill, salt and pepper. Cover with water and simmer until the carrots are tender.

5 When almost cooked prepare the egg-lemon sauce: in a deep bowl beat the egg well.

6 Squeeze the lemon and remove any pips. Add the juice with salt and pepper to the egg beating continuously. Then add the cornflour that has been dissolved in a little cold water.

7 Take a little of the hot vegetable 'broth' and gradually pour this into the egg-lemon mixture, while stirring continuously.

8 Remove the saucepan from the heat and pour in the egg-lemon sauce, shake the pan to ensure that it mixes in well. Leave to stand for a while until the sauce is smooth and thick.

Leek tart *(tarte me prassa)*

Ingredients

For the pastry:
300g plain flour
150g cold butter
1 egg
½ cup grated parmesan (optional)
A little cold beer or soda water
A little salt/freshly ground pepper

For the filling:
4 medium sized leeks
½ cup olive oil
1 tsp sugar
2 eggs
200g soft yellow cheese
200g fresh cream
½ tsp nutmeg (optional)
Salt/freshly ground black pepper

1 Sift the flour into a large bowl, add the diced butter and rub in with fingertips until the mixture resembles fine breadcrumbs. Stir in a pinch of salt, some pepper and the parmesan.

2 Add the egg and using a knife stir in gradually just enough beer (or soda water) and mix to a firm *dough*. Knead the *dough* briefly and gently on a floured surface.

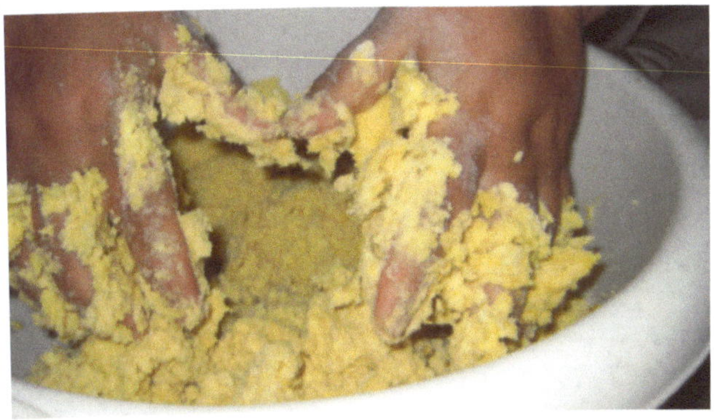

3 Place the dough into a 25cm loose-bottomed tart tin and slowly spread it out by hand making sure that the bottom and sides are well lined. Prick the surface of the dough to prevent it from bubbling while it is baking.

4 Bake at 180°C for about 15 minutes until the dough is dry and half cooked.

5 Meanwhile, wash and cut the leeks into slices.

6 Heat the oil in a frying pan and stir fry the leeks until soft. Add salt, pepper, nutmeg and sugar. Mix well and cook until the liquid has evaporated, and the leeks are a light brown colour. It is very important not to have any liquid.

7 Remove from the heat and add the eggs, cheese and fresh cream mixing well. Pour the mixture into the pastry case and then bake in the oven at 180°C for about an hour until the surface of the tart has a light brown crust.

Spinach pie *(spanakopita)*

Notes: Greek pies constitute a great tradition and always carry a celebratory nuance.

– In Greece *spanakopita* is generally served cool or at room temperature.
– The recipe given here includes homemade pastry but as Daphne points out bought *fyllo* pastry is an alternative although not as good: use 5-6 sheets at the bottom (brushing each sheet with oil before placing the next one) and 4-5 sheets for the top.

Ingredients

For the pastry:
4-4½ cups self-raising flour
1½-1¾ cups warm water
1 tbsp olive oil
1½ cups melted butter
½ tsp salt

For the filling:
1-1½kg spinach
4 eggs
350g feta
3-4 medium sized onions
1 bunch dill
4-5 spring onions
½ cup olive oil
Salt/freshly ground black pepper

Preparing the pastry:

1 Mix together the flour and salt in a large bowl. Make a well in the centre and add the water and oil, mixing slowly by hand from the centre to the sides. Knead for about 10 minutes until the dough is good and elastic.

2 Divide the dough into two balls. Cover and leave to rest for about 30 minutes. Flatten the first balls by pressing between the palms to form a circular shape. Place on a floured board and with a rolling-pin roll out to a circle of 50-60cm diameter

3 Place a small plate (or saucer) in the centre of the dough and brush with the melted butter the surfaces not covered by the plate. With a sharp knife make cuts outwards from the plate to form 8 equal parts or petals.

4 Remove the plate and begin to fold the sections of dough towards the centre one at a time. Brush the exposed surfaced with the melted butter.

5 Cover with a clean cloth and allow to rest for about 20 minutes at room temperature. Repeat this procedure with the second ball of dough.
Note: the dough can be prepared the day before and stored in the fridge wrapped in clingfilm but must be allowed to get to room temperature before it is rolled out.

Preparing the filling:

1 Wash and rinse the spinach well, then chop it, place it in a deep bowl and sprinkle it with salt.

2 Squeeze out as much water as possible by hand or use a salad spinner (dryer) and put the strained spinach into a deep bowl.

3 Finely chop the onions, spring onions and dill. Mash the feta with a fork. Add all of this together with the eggs, olive oil, salt and pepper to the bowl with the spinach and mix well.
Note: Be careful with the amount of salt that is added because feta is a salty cheese.

Now to assemble the pie:

1 Brush an oven dish lightly with oil.

2 Take one ball of dough and with a rolling pin roll it out on a lightly floured surface. It should be slightly larger in size than the dish.

3 Pick up the pastry (using a rolling pin if the pastry is a bit delicate) and drape over the oven dish. Gently mould the pastry into the dish and pour in the filling.

4 Roll out the other ball of dough and place this on top of the dish. Make sure that the edges of the top and bottom layers of pastry meet. This allows the edges to be sealed so that the filling does not seep out.

5 To indicate how the pie is to be cut up at the end score the top of the pastry into diamond or square shapes.

6 Bake in a pre-heated oven at 180°C for about an hour or until the is nicely brown. Serve at room temperature.

Note: Daphne explains that during the summer months in Greece one cannot find fresh spinach, so they have to use it frozen. To make the filling is slightly different. In a pan heat a ¼ cup of olive oil, lightly fry the chopped onions and then add the spring onions. Next, add the frozen spinach cut coarsely and stir until all the liquid has evaporated. If necessary, throw off some of the liquid. Take off the heat and add the crumbled feta cheese, add some more olive oil, the dill, eggs, salt and pepper.

Zucchini (courgette) pie
(kolokithopita)

Note: See the notes for spinach pie on page 56.

Ingredients *(serves 4)*

For the pastry:
500g self-raising flour
½ cup olive oil
1 tsp salt
Water

For the filling:
4-5 medium sized zucchini
1 large onion
1 bunch dill
¾ cup olive oil
3 eggs
400g feta
Salt/freshly ground black pepper

1 In a bowl mix the flour, salt and half cup of oil. Slowly add water, stirring continuously until you have a batter a little thicker than a pancake batter. Leave to stand for a while and prepare the filling.

2 Wash and grate the zucchini. Squeeze very well to get as much water out as possible.

3 Finely chop the onion and dill. Crumble the feta. Mix these with the zucchini, add the eggs and season with salt and pepper.

4 Oil the oven dish and put in two-thirds of the batter, spreading it evenly so that the whole base of the dish is covered.

5 Carefully pour the filling on top of the batter, and then pour the remaining batter on top of this to cover the whole pie.

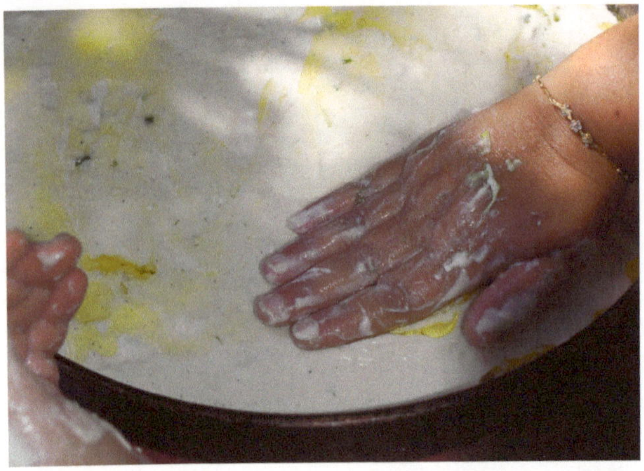

6 Sprinkle the remaining olive oil over the pie and bake in a preheated oven at 180°C for about 45 minutes.

Chickpeas in the oven *(revithia sto fourno)*

Ingredients (serves 4)

500g chickpeas
2 onions
2 tomatoes
2-3 bay leaves
1-2 handfuls rosemary
2 garlic cloves
½-¾ cup olive oil
Salt/freshly ground black pepper

1 Put the chickpeas into a bowl, cover with water and allow to soak overnight.

2 In the morning strain and rub gently to remove the husks.

3 Cut the onions and tomatoes into slices. Cut the garlic into thin slices.

4 Put the chickpeas into a deep oven dish (preferably one with a lid).

5 Layer the sliced tomatoes, onions and garlic on top of the chickpeas.

6 Sprinkle the rosemary over the top.

7 Add the bay leaves, salt, pepper and oil.

8 Cover all with water.

9 If the over dish does not have a lid cover it tightly with foil.

10 Bake at 170°C for about 3 hours.

11 Uncover the dish for the last 20 minutes.

Daphne says that all the recipes she has seen advise one to add baking soda to the water when soaking the chickpeas overnight. She tried this but found that while the chickpeas were softer, they had an unpleasant smell.

Runner beans in tomato sauce
(fasolakia)

Ingredients

1 kg fresh beans
2 potatoes
1-2 carrots
1 large onion
1 bunch parsley
¾ cup olive oil
1 tin (400g) chopped tomatoes (or tomato passata)
1 teaspoon sugar
Salt/freshly ground black pepper

1 Wash the beans well and remove any strings.

2 Finely chop the parsley.

3 Wash, peel and cut the carrot into thin slices'

4 Finely chop the onion by hand or briefly in a food processor.

5 Peel, wash and cut the potatoes into medium size pieces.

6 Place oil in deep pan and heat. When hot add the onion and fry lightly until soft.

7 Add the beans, potatoes and carrots and fry lightly for two minutes while stirring.

8 Pour in the tin of tomato and add the same amount of water.

9 Add the salt, pepper, sugar and parsley and stir well.

10 Cook over medium heat for about an hour. When the dish is ready it should have some sauce but there should not be too much liquid.

As Daphne points out, when there are no fresh beans available one can use frozen ones. They can be added to the pan without defrosting them and cooked in the same way but with less water and for a shorter time.

Stuffed aubergines *(skafoudes)*

Notes:
– Daphne explains that *skafoudes* is what Lesvians call small boats or small tubs for washing clothes in.
– If prepared in the same way but with mince meat added, then they are called *papoutsakia* which means 'small shoes.' See page 116.

Ingredients

6-8 large aubergines (same size ideally)
2 onions
2 ripe tomatoes
2 eggs
½ cup yellow medium hard cheese
½ cup feta cheese (optional)
1 bunch parsley
½-¾ cup olive oil
Salt/freshly ground black pepper

1 Wash the aubergines and cut them in half lengthways, keeping the stalk.

2 Cook them in a big pan of slightly salted boiling water until soft. Then take them out and drain.

3 Using a spoon scoop some of the pulp out from the middle taking care not to split the walls of the aubergines.

4 Grate the yellow cheese then finely chop the onions, tomatoes and parsley.

5 In a pan heat the oil and sauté the onions lightly. Add the removed pulp, tomatoes, parsley, salt and pepper. Cook until the water has gone and the sauce has thickened.

6 Remove from the heat. Add the grated cheese, feta, and the 2 egg yolks to the mixture and stir in.

7 Place the aubergine halves in an oven dish that has been generously brushed with oil. Fill each half with the mixture.

8 Beat the egg whites with a little salt and cover the top of each aubergine with this, which forms a crust when cooked.

9 Bake in a preheated oven at 180°C for about an hour until golden brown.

10 Serve hot or cold.

Aubergines in tomato sauce
(melitzanes me saltsa domata)

Ingredients

5-6 aubergines
½ bunch parsley (optional)
Oil (olive or sunflower) for frying

For the sauce:
5-6 ripe tomatoes grated (no skins)
1 tbsp sugar
½ cup olive oil
Salt/freshly ground black pepper

1 Wash and peel the aubergines zebra style. In this way some of the bitter flavour of the skin is maintained without overpowering the dish.

2 Cut into slices and fry these in hot oil.

3 Remove from the heat and lay the slices on absorbent paper to take up the excess oil.

4 Put the tomato, olive oil, sugar, salt and pepper into a deep frying pan and mix it all well.

5 Cook the sauce until the water has evaporated and it has thickened.

6 Put the fried aubergine slices into the sauce and bring it to the boil.

7 Remove from the heat and leave it to cool. Serve either warm or cool and sprinkle with parsley (optional).

Aubergines with yogurt
(melitzanes me yiaourti)

Note: Daphne says that if one fries the aubergines first one will get a more traditional taste, but the dish will become heavier because the aubergines absorb a lot of oil.

Ingredients

5-6 medium sized aubergines
2 onions
1 bunch parsley
2-3 garlic cloves
1½ tins (400+200 g) chopped tomatoes
1 tbsp sugar
1 cup olive oil
Oregano (optional)
Salt/freshly ground black pepper
250 g Greek yogurt
Paprika (powder)

1 Wash the aubergines and then cut them into cubes.

2 Finely chop the parsley, onions and garlic.

3 Put the aubergines in an oven dish and add the onions, garlic, salt, pepper, oregano, chopped tomato, sugar, parsley and oil. Mix well.

5 Bake in the oven at 180°C until the aubergines are soft and the sauce has thickened.

6 Place the aubergines in a dish and when cool spread a layer of yogurt over the top. Before serving sprinkle with sweet red paprika.

Vegetarian dolmades *(dolmadakia yialantzi)*

Notes:

– Daphne explains that these *dolmades yialantzi* are the ones without mince-meat. 'Yialan' in Turkish means "a lie", so they are fake *dolmades*. See page 151 for the version with meat stuffing.

– Vine leaves are commonly harvested from wild vines, rather than the plants farmed for winemaking, because they are generally more tender and have more flavour. If one does not have fresh vine leaves available, it is possible to buy them in resealable packs that are ideal if one only makes some *dolmades* occasionally. They are very easy to use, as you can take out a few leaves at a time and keep the rest for another day. The pack will keep in the fridge for a few weeks.

– Vine leaves in brine are also available. These are great if you want to start cooking right away, as the leaves are already nice and soft. Simply rinse off the brine and you're ready to go!

Ingredients (about 6+ servings)
500 g fresh vine leaves
2 onions
4-5 spring onions
1 zucchini
Some lettuce leaves
3-4 tbsp mint
3-4 tbsp parsley
3-4 tbsp dill
1½ cups good quality olive oil
1-1½ cups of risotto rice
1 lemon
Salt/freshly ground black pepper

1 Put the vine leaves into boiling water for about a minute. When they have changed colour take them out with a perforated spoon and leave them to cool. Be careful not to let them boil as them may disintegrate and be difficult to handle.

2 Finely chop the onions, spring onions, lettuce, parsley, mint and dill.

3 Grate the zucchini and squeeze the lemon removing any pips.

4 In a bowl mix all the ingredients: onions, spring onions, zucchini, lettuce, mint, dill, parsley, rice, 1 cup of oil, lemon juice, salt and pepper.

5 Line the bottom of a saucepan with some of the vine leaves so that the *dolmades* do not stick. This is one way of using any damaged leaves.

6 Take a leaf and place a teaspoon of the filling just above the base of the leaf. Fold the base of the leaf over the filling, then fold in the sides and then roll to the end of the leaf so you have a neat, tight parcel.

7 Arrange the *dolmades* next to each other, without any space between them and the open sides underneath, in the saucepan.

8 Carefully pour enough water into the saucepan to cover the *dolmades* and add the remaining half cup of oil.

9 Place a plate over the *dolmades* to prevent them from unwrapping or moving about in the saucepan.

10 Cook on a medium heat until all the liquid has been absorbed.

11 Leave to cool and serve them warm. In Greece they are very often served with thick plain yogurt as a *meze*. They may of course be used as a first course or as part of the main course.

Note:
If folding and rolling the *dolmades* proves difficult it is even possible to buy an inexpensive 'machine' to help, and these can be found quite easily online.

Lemon potatoes *(patates lemonates)*

Ingredients

1 kg waxy potatoes
1 tbsp oregano
Extra virgin olive oil
Juice of 2 lemons
Salt

1 Preheat the oven to 200°C.

2 Peel and wash the potatoes and then cut them lengthways into narrow fingers of approximately the same size so that they all cook at the same rate.

3 Arrange the potatoes as flat as possible over the bottom of an oven-proof dish, season with salt and the oregano, and drizzle with olive oil. The oil is important for the roasting, but the amount can vary according to taste. Pour the lemon juice evenly over the potatoes and then pour over sufficient water to just cover them.

4 Bake until the water has evaporated. To brown the top, drizzle with more olive oil. When brown turn off the oven and leave the potatoes in the oven to stand for a few minutes more.

Potato 'stew' *(patates yiachni)*

Note: This traditional, rustic potato stew recipe is an excellent example of how Greek cuisine takes the simplest ingredients and transforms them effortlessly into a tasty dish! In Greece and Turkey, the cooking technique known as *yiachni* refers to any vegetables (notably green beans and potatoes) stewed simply with onions, tomato, garlic, herbs and lashings of olive oil. Vegetables *yiachni* are often made during Greek Orthodox fasting periods, when many Orthodox Christians exclude meat (and dairy products) from their diets. Since Orthodox fasting days comprise nearly half the year's calendar, *yiachni* appears frequently on the dinner tables of the devout.

Ingredients
1 kg potatoes
2 medium onions
1 tin (400 g) chopped tomatoes
½ bunch parsley
1 tsp sugar
½ cup olive oil
2 bay leaves (optional)
A pinch of allspice (optional)
Salt/freshly ground black pepper

1 Peel, wash and cut the potatoes in medium sized pieces.

2 Cut the onions into slices.

3 Heat the oil in a deep saucepan and then lightly fry the onion until soft and light brown.
Add the potatoes and mix well with a with a wooden spoon.

4 Add the tomatoes, salt, pepper, sugar and (optional) a little more oil, bay leaves and a pinch of allspice.

5 Top up with water until the potatoes are covered. Cook on a medium heat until the potatoes are soft, and the sauce has thickened.

Notes:
– Daphne usually makes this for an evening family meal with a slice of feta cheese on the side, which adds to the taste. She also says that for a change it can be baked in the oven. It only needs more time.
– Some people feel fresh, ripe tomatoes are a must and some add garlic. There are those who think that while not very common in Greece, adding some good quality Kalamata olives and vegetable stock gives a really deep unique taste.

Spinach rice *(spanakorizo)*

Ingredients (serves about 4)

1 kg spinach
1½ cups risotto rice
1 large onion
3-4 spring onions with stalks
1 bunch dill
½ cup olive oil
1 lemon
Salt/freshly ground black pepper

1 Wash the spinach well, dry and then chop it. Finely chop the onion and spring onions.

2 Heat oil in a deep pan and lightly sauté the onion and spring onions. Add the spinach and stir for a few minutes.

3 Add rice, salt, pepper and enough water to cook the rice keeping in mind that the spinach will shed some too. Bring to a simmer on a low heat and stir so that it does not stick to pan.

4 Finely chop the dill and squeeze the lemon. When rice is nearly ready take off the heat and add these. Cover and let stand in the pan for 5 minutes.

Cabbage rice *(lachanorizo)*

Notes:
– Dishes of vegetables and greens combined with rice make good vegetarian meals and are common in Greek households especially on the days they are supposed to abstain from meat according to Orthodox tradition.
– Daphne believes that these rice dishes are best served with feta and black olives. However, to provide for a more substantial non-vegetarian meal they may be supplemented with something else such as *keftedes* or fried fish.

Ingredients

½ a white cabbage
1½ cups of risotto rice
2 onions
1 big carrot
1 bunch parsley
½ cup olive oil
1 lemon
Salt/freshly ground black pepper

1 Take the outside leaves of the cabbage, wash and cut into large chunky pieces.

2 Finely chop the onion and carrot.

3 Heat the oil in a saucepan and lightly fry the onion and carrot.

4 Add the cabbage and stir until it has softened. Add, rice, salt, pepper and as much water as needed for the rice to cook.

5 Lower the heat and allow to simmer stirring occasionally.

6 Finely chop the parsley and squeeze the lemon.

7 When the rice is nearly ready take off the heat. Add the parsley and lemon juice.

8 Cover the pan and allow it to stand for 5 minutes before serving.

Notes:
– Daphne points out that leek rice (or leek combined with cabbage) can be prepared in the same way.
– An even tastier version of this dish is common in Thrace (NE of Greek mainland), where they add some tomato passata instead of lemon juice and add ½ a cup of currants, ½ a cup of coarsely chopped walnuts and 1 tsp of cumin or cinnamon.

Lentil soup *(fakes)*

Notes:
– This thick peasant soup is eaten all over Greece, winter and summer, and particularly during lent.
– Daphne explains that vinegar is essential not only for the taste but also to make it digestible. If someone does not like, or is not allowed to eat, vinegar each person can add it to their soup when it is served.
– Lentils are usually served with feta, olives and fresh bread.
– The nutty flavour of the lentils, that combines well with garlic, onions and tomato, will develop even better if it is reheated.

Ingredients

500 g lentils (medium size)
1-2 big onions
1-2 garlic cloves
1 big potato
1 big carrot
1 tin (400 g) chopped tomatoes
2 bay leaves
2 tsp oregano (dried)
½ cup olive oil
1 tbsp vinegar
Salt/freshly ground black pepper

1 Wash the lentils in a colander. Put them into a saucepan and cover them well with water. Boil for a short time and then drain the water.

2 Add fresh hot water to about 3-4 cm above the beans and bring to the boil.

3 Peel, wash and cut the potato into cubes.

4 Peel, wash and finely slice the carrot.

5 Cut the onion into chunks and finely chop the garlic.

6 To the saucepan add the potato, carrot, garlic and chopped tomatoes. Season with salt and pepper, add the oregano and bay leaves.

7 Add vinegar and olive oil. Both can be added now or at the end of cooking.

8 The soup is ready when it has thickened, and the lentils have softened. If the consistency is not thick enough one can put a few spoonfuls of the lentils in a blender to make a thick smooth paste that can be added back to the soup.

Cannellini bean soup *(fasolada)*

Notes:
– The simple *fasolada* was for centuries the Greek national dish. As Daphne explains one can imagine how easy it was to feed a large family by adding to the soup several available vegetables and sometimes a small piece of meat or sausage. The art of turning simplicity into a delicacy is passed on from mother to daughter.
– This dish is traditionally served with olives, feta cheese, onions and smoked herring or *taramosalata* and, of course, fresh bread.

Ingredients

500 g cannellini beans
2 large onions
1 celery stalk
2-3 carrots
1 tin (400 g) chopped tomatoes
1 red pepper
1 chilli pepper (optional)
½ cup olive oil
Salt/freshly ground black pepper

1 Put the beans in a bowl covered with cold water and leave them to soak overnight.

2 Rinse the beans in a colander, then put them into a large saucepan and cover with fresh water.

3 Boil for a short time then drain off the water.

4 Refill the pan with hot water to about 3-4 cm above the beans and bring to the boil.

5 Meanwhile chop the onion and peel, wash, and cut the carrots into slices. Deseed the pepper and cut into large pieces.

6 Add the vegetables to the pan, including the celery stalk that can be removed after cooking.

7 Season with salt and pepper.

8 Add the oil — it can be done at this stage or at the beginning of the cooking.

9 The soup is ready when it has thickened, and the beans have softened. If the consistency is not thick enough one can put a few spoonfuls of the beans in a blender to make a thick smooth paste that can be added back to the soup.

Note: Soups, many of them based on pulses, are generally very popular in Greece, particularly in winter. One advantage is that they tend to be even more intense in flavour on the second or even the third day.

Above: An example of *fasolada*.

Below: Chickpea soup, another great favourite with Greeks.

Chickpea soup *(revithosoupa)*

Note: Long, slow cooking, with the soup simmering gently, allows a gradual and wonderful amalgamation of all the ingredients.

Ingredients
500 g chickpeas
1-2 onions
1-2 lemons
¾ cup olive oil
1½ tsp cornflour
Salt/freshly ground black pepper

1 The night before, place the chickpeas in a deep bowl and cover with water. Allow them to soak overnight.

2 In the morning strain and gently rub the chickpeas to remove the husks.

3 Finely chop the onions.

4 In a large saucepan put about 2 litres of water then add the chickpeas and onion.

5 Simmer on a medium heat for about 1½ hours until the chickpeas are very soft.

6 Squeeze the lemons and dilute the cornflour in a little cold water.

7 Add the lemon juice, oil, cornflower, salt and pepper and stir well.

8 Bring the soup to the boil briefly, and cook until it has thickened. If it is still rather watery one can put a few spoonfuls of the peas in a blender and then add them back to the soup.

Lentil salad *(fakosalata)*

Note: The lentil plant (Lens Culinaris) originates from Asia and North Africa and is one of our oldest sources of food. A cousin to the pea and a rich provider of protein and carbohydrates, the lentil is also a good source of calcium, phosphorus, iron and B vitamins — making it an important diet staple the world over. There are several types , but the small brown ones are the most popular in Greece.

***Ingredients** (serves 4)*

500 g lentils
2 bay leaves
2 garlic cloves
1 cup celery (finely chopped)
1 cup onion (finely chopped)
1 cup chopped walnuts
1 red pepper
Salt

Dressing:
1 cup olive oil
2 tbsp balsamic vinegar
1 tbsp sugar or honey
2 garlic cloves
1 tbsp mustard
Juice of half a lemon

1 Wash lentils in a colander and put them into a saucepan covered with water.

2 Add bay leaves and garlic then boil until lentils are fairly soft.

3 Rinse lentils in a colander and then leave them to cool in a large bowl.

4 Core the red pepper and cut it into smallish pieces.

5 Add the red pepper, onion, celery and walnuts to the lentils and mix it all well.

6 In a food blender combine the oil, vinegar, sugar, garlic, mustard and lemon juice until smooth. Pour over the lentils and mix well.

Black-eyed bean salad *(fasolia mavromitika)*

Ingredients

2 cups dry black-eyed beans
5-6 tbsp olive oil
3-4 tbsp lemon juice
3 tbsp finely chopped walnuts
1 garlic clove crushed
¾ cup parsley (chopped)
¾ cup rocket (chopped)
¼ cup pomegranate (optional)
Salt/freshly ground black

1 Put the beans in a saucepan, cover them with cold water and bring to the boil for 5 minutes.

2 Strain off the water and recover the beans with fresh water. Cover the saucepan and cook for about 20-30 minutes until the beans are soft. Be careful not to overcook because the beans can become quite mushy.

3 Drain the beans through a colander and place them in a bowl allowing them to reach room temperature.

4 Add the parsley and rocket to the beans.

5 In another bowl mix the oil, lemon juice, walnuts, garlic and season with salt and pepper.

6 Pour the dressing over the beans and mix gently, but well, with a spoon. The salad can be garnished with pomegranate seeds.

Daphne's potatoes

Note: Daphne suggests that instead of an oven dish one can use small separate oven proof bowls.

***Ingredients** (serves 4)*

1 kg potatoes
1 bunch parsley
3-4 garlic cloves
1 tin cut mushrooms (350 g strained)
350 g soft yellow cheese
1 beef cube
250 g fresh cream
Salt/freshly ground black pepper
Vegetable oil for frying

1 Peel, wash and cut the potatoes into 1cm thick slices.

2 In a frying pan heat the oil and fry the sliced potatoes until soft or light brown. Set aside.

3 With a little oil (add some if needed) lightly fry the mushrooms in the same pan. Add the crumbled beef cube and stir until the cube has melted and the mushrooms no longer have any liquid.

4 Mix the parsley and garlic in a food processor.

5 Grate the cheese (if not already grated).

6 In an oven dish put a layer of half the potatoes, season with salt and pepper and then add half the mushrooms on top of this.

7 Over this sprinkle half the parsley and garlic mixture.

8 Sprinkle half the cheese over this.

9 Now repeat steps 6,7 and 8 using the remaining ingredients.

10 Finish by pouring the fresh cream over the dish.

11 Bake in a preheated oven at 180ºC for about 30 minutes until the top has a golden crust.

Aubergine rolls

Ingredients

2 aubergines
1 tomato
100 g feta
Some currants
Zest of half a lemon
1 handful of parsley (or basil)
1-2 garlic cloves (optional)
Little olive oil

1 Wash the aubergines and cut them into about 1cm thick slices lengthways. Discard the outer slices.

2 Layer the slices in an oiled oven dish. Sprinkle with salt and brush with olive oil. Bake in the oven at 180°C for about 20 minutes until softened and golden brown.

3 Take the aubergine slices out and while they are cooling prepare the filling.

4 Finely chop the tomato and the parsley. Crumble the feta.

5 Lightly mix together the chopped tomato and parley, the feta, currants, lemon zest, olive oil and crushed garlic if it is being used.

6 On a baked aubergine slice put a small spoonful of the filling (the amount depends on the size of the aubergine) and do **not** spread it over the slice. Roll the slice around the filling.

7 Repeat the above process with all the slices. Put all the rolls into an oven dish and then into the hot oven at 180°C for about 10 minutes.

Votsala rice salad

Ingredients

1 onion finely chopped
1 apple finely chopped
2 carrots grated
1 handful raisins/currants
Curry, salt, pepper, according to taste
Olive oil
2 cups rice/4 cups water

1 Heat the oil and then sauté the onions and carrots.

2 Add the rice, apple and currants. Then add the water and mix everything well.

3 Add the curry, salt and pepper to taste.

4 Boil until all the water has been absorbed.

Votsala pasta salad

Ingredients
2 cups farfalle pasta
4 cups water
For the sauce/dressing
1 tomato
1 garlic clove
50 gr feta cheese
Some fresh basil and oregano leaves
2 tbs olive oil
Some chopped tomato and crumbled feta for garnish

1 Add the pasta to boiling water. The water may cool slightly so it is important to continue to cook on high until the water comes to a full boil again. Then the heat should be turned down slightly but left high enough for the water to maintain a steady boil.

2 The pasta should be cooked to an "al dente" state and not allowed to become too soft. When done, strain and allow it to cool down.

3 In a food processor mix the ingredients for the dressing carefully, not allowing them to become too liquid. The sauce should be thick and chunky.

4 Pour this over the pasta and toss. Garnish with some chopped tomato and crumbled feta.

Votsala avocado salad

Note: In Greece *kritharaki* rice shaped pasta (see *youvetsi* on page 98) is used but any kind of small-sized pasta can be used instead.

Ingredients
1 cup orzo
1 red/yellow pepper finely chopped
1 avocado cut in chunky pieces
1/2 onion finely chopped
1 handful celery leaves finely chopped
1 cup red beans (canned)
2 slices of ham/ optional
Dressing (equal portions of the following)
Balsamic vinegar
Honey
Mustard
Olive oil

1 Boil the pasta in water, not letting it get too soft. Drain and rinse in a colander and allow it to cool.

2 Meanwhile cut up the pepper, avocado, onion, celery and ham if it is used. In a large bowl add these to the pasta together with the beans and mix it all well.

3 Mix the dressing ingredients and pour over the salad. Some grated parmesan, or other hard cheese can be used as a garnish.

Note: Left top photo is the Votsala pasta salad. The two other photos are of the avocado salad.

Meat *(kreas)*

In the home meat plays an important, though small, part in the family's diet. In traditional Greek cooking meat is not daily fare, it symbolizes rather celebration and gratitude, and is the food for special occasions. As part of traditions that go back to ancient Greece lamb is roasted for the biggest religious or family feasts: Easter, name days, holidays, weddings, baptisms, and Sundays. As Rena Salaman writes in her book *'Greek Food'*: "Tender, young, succulent lamb is the king of every Greek feast, preferably roasted whole on an outdoor spit, or stuffed with fried onions, minced meat, and pine nuts and roasted in a large, shallow oven dish in the local baker's."

At Christmas pork tends to be eaten. In some parts of the country it was the main meat, and families would feed a pig with the leftovers from their own tables, plus choice titbits, for a whole year. They were usually slaughtered on the first cold days of November when they were fat enough, and the salted meat, lard, sausages and pickled cuts would feed them for an entire year.

Although grilled chops and kebabs (*souvlakia*) are popular, the cuisine involves more stews and casseroles than whole joints. Oven-baked dishes, ideally in a clay pot, when the meat simmers gently and slowly in its own juices, are enhanced with herbs, spices and vegetables; the result is meltingly tender meat covered with a thick aromatic sauce.

Pork roll with feta *(hirino rolo me feta)*

Ingredients

1-1½ kg pork shoulder or leg
300 g feta cheese
2-3 tomatoes
2-3 peppers
½ cup olive oil
2 tbsp sweet paprika
2 tbsp oregano
Garlic granules
Salt/freshly ground black pepper

1 When buying the pork ask the butcher to cut it into slices as large as possible so that it can be rolled up.

2 Crumble the feta or mash it with a fork. Cut the tomatoes and peppers into slices.

3 In a bowl mix the olive oil, oregano, paprika, salt, pepper and garlic granules. Lay out the pork and brush it well with part of this mixture.

4 In the centre of the pork, length wise, place some feta and on top of this peppers and tomato. Over this pour some of the oil mixture.

5 Roll up the meat using toothpicks to hold it in place, and brush the outside well with the remaining oil mixture.

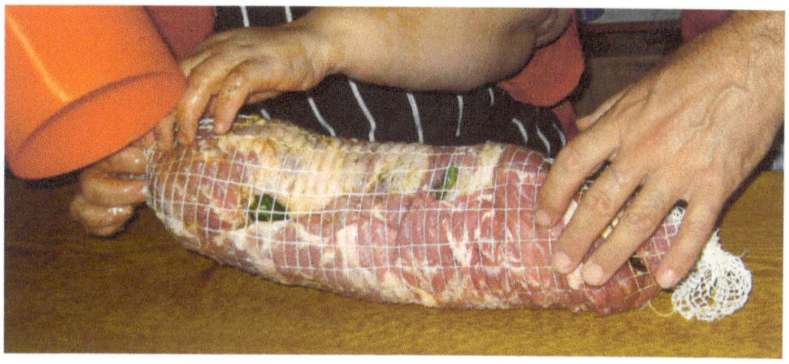

6 Preheat oven to 180°C. Put the rolled pork into an oiled oven dish together with a cup of water and cook for about 2-2½ hours at 170°C. Note: the meat juices can be used as a base for gravy by boiling it while stirring constantly and slowly adding cornflour dissolved in cold water.

Chicken with feta *(kotopoulo me feta)*

Ingredients

700 g chicken breasts
2 ripe tomatoes
2 green peppers
150-200 g feta cheese
1 large onion
1 garlic clove
½ cup olive oil
½ bunch parsley
1 handful mint
1 tsp sugar
Salt/freshly ground black pepper

1 Wash the chicken well and cut it into large cubes.

2 Finely chop the onion, parsley, garlic and mint. Slice the tomatoes and cut the peppers into chunks.

3 Heat oil in a saucepan, add the chicken, and fry until it is brown all around.

4 Add onion and garlic then fry lightly.

5 On top of the chicken, layer the sliced tomato and peppers.

6 Carefully sprinkle with a little salt (the feta is salty), pepper and the sugar. If necessary, add a little water.

7 Lower the heat and let it simmer. When nearly ready crumble the feta by hand and add it. Sprinkle some parsley and mint over the top.

8 Allow to cook until the sauce has thickened. Note: if too much liquid, it can be thickened by adding (stirred well) one tablespoon of cornflour dissolved in a little cold water.

Stuffed cabbage leaves
(lahanodolmades)

Note: In Greece the white Dutch cabbage is used, but in some places, e.g. the UK, a green type may be better.

Ingredients
1 white cabbage (medium sized)
½ kg beef mince
¾ cup risotto rice
1 onion
2-3 spring onions
½ bunch parsley
Some mint
½ tsp cumin
½ cup olive oil
Salt/freshly ground black pepper

For the egg-lemon sauce:
2 eggs
1 lemon (juice)
1 tbsp corn flower
Salt/freshly ground black pepper

1 With a sharp knife remove the hard core of the cabbage.

2 Put the cabbage into a deep saucepan of salted water and boil whole.

3 When it has softened take it out of the pan to cool off.

4 *Meanwhile prepare the filling:* place the mince in a bowl, add the rice, and the finely chopped onion, spring onion (including the green stalks), parsley and mint.

5 Add cumin, oil, salt and pepper.

6 Peel off the cabbage leaves and keep some of the harder leaves to the side.

7 Cut away the hard stalks of the leaves and finely chop some of the stalks (1 cup).

8 Add the cup of chopped stalks to the bowl of filling and mix all the ingredients very well.

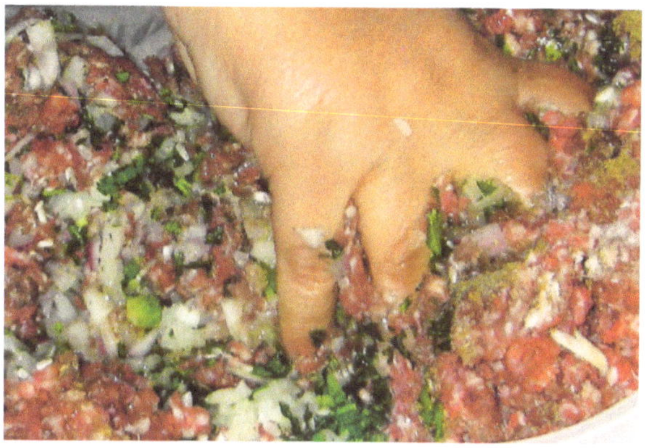

9 Place a tablespoon of the filling at the end of each leaf and fold them over carefully and tightly. Do this gently, taking care not to tear the leaves (if some are too big cut them in half).

10 On the bottom of the deep saucepan arrange the hard, outer leaves that have been kept aside, in order to prevent the *dolmades* from sticking. Layer them tightly together in circles with the seams facing downward. Try not to have more than 2-3 layers.

11 Cover the *dolmades* with water and put a plate on top to stop to stop them dancing about while they are cooking. Cover the saucepan and cook for about 1 hour on a low heat.

When almost cooked prepare the egg-lemon sauce:

1 In a bowl beat the eggs very well. Squeeze the lemon and remove any pips.

2 Add the lemon juice to the eggs together with a little salt and pepper beating continuously.

3 Then blend the cornflour with two parts cold water until smooth and stir the mixture into the sauce.

4 Take about 4-5 tablespoons of the hot liquid from the saucepan of the cooked *dolmades* and add this to the egg-lemon sauce gradually stirring continuously.

5 Turn off the heat and pour the egg-lemon sauce over the *dolmades*. Shake the saucepan to ensure that the sauce mixes in throughout. Leave it to stand for a while to allow the *dolmades* to blend with the sauce.

Meatballs in egg-lemon sauce *(youvarlakia)*

Ingredients

1 kg beef mince
¾ cup risotto rice
1 onion
½ cup mint
½ bunch parsley
½ cup olive oil
1 egg
Salt/freshly ground black pepper

For the egg-lemon sauce:
2 eggs
1 lemon
1 tbsp cornflour
Salt/freshly ground black pepper

1 Finely chop the onion, mint and parsley.

2 Put the mince into a bowl and add the onion, mint, parsley, rice, oil, eggs, salt and pepper. Mix all these ingredients well.

3 Divide the mixture into smallish round meatballs and put them into a deep saucepan.

4 Cover with water and cook for about 30 minutes on a medium heat.

5 When the meatballs are almost cooked prepare the egg-lemon sauce all as described on page 84.

6 Take the meatballs off the heat and pour in the egg-lemon sauce shaking the saucepan in order to ensure that the sauce mixes in well everywhere.

7 Leave it to stand for a while until the sauce is smooth and thick.

Hünkar Beğendi *(the emperor's favourite dish)*

Notes:

– In Turkey it seems that this is traditionally a rich lamb stew with aubergine purée. Daphne's recipe is based on the beloved classic Greek beef stew *kokkinisto,* which means 'reddened', and describes a dish that has been slowly cooked in a red wine and tomato sauce.

– Daphne tells the following story: when Empress Eugenie, the wife of Napoleon III, visited the Topkapi palace in Istanbul in the mid-19th century, the Sultan's chef had the idea to combine the usual "*kokkinisto*" (beef in tomato sauce) with an aubergine purée. As he explained later, he had been told that in France they eat everything in purée form! The two parts are cook separately and only at the end they are served together.

Ingredients

1-1½ Kg beef (or lamb)
2 large onions
½ cup of olive oil
¾ cup of red wine
1½ tins (400+200 g) chopped tomatoes or tomato passata
1-2 tsp of sugar
2 bay leaves
4-5 allspice berries (optional)
1 cinnamon stick (optional)
Salt/freshly ground black pepper

For the aubergine purée:

5-6 big aubergines
1½ cups fresh cream
2 cups yellow cheese (grated)
1 tbsp of butter
Smoked salt

1 Finely chop the onions.

2 Heat oil and brown the meat on all sides in batches and then take out of pan.

3 Sautee the onion in the pan until golden and then put back the meat.

4 Add wine, stir meat in the pan, and add 2 cups of water.

5 Cook at a low heat, and after a while add bay leaves, allspice, cinnamon stick and pepper.

6 When the meat is almost tender add the tomatoes, sugar and salt, then cook until the sauce thickens. It should be rich and thick. If it is too runny, remove the meat and reduce the liquid a little, return the meat to the pan and warm through.

Aubergine purée:

1 Wash the aubergines and place them whole into an oven dish.

2 Bake in a hot oven at 180°C until soft.

Note:
Traditionally one aubergine is grilled or burnt over a flame blackened to give add a smoked flavour. Alternatively one can use smoked salt.

3 Take the aubergines out of the oven, cut into halves and leave to cool.

4 Using a spoon, remove the inner part and place in a food processor (remove big seeds if too many). Some people feel that done this way the purée becomes too smooth and feel it is better when mashed with a fork.

5 Put the purée into a pan add butter, cheese and salt.

6 Cook over a low heat, stirring continuously, until the cheese has melted.

7 Pour in cream and stir for a couple of minutes then take off the heat. The amount of cream used depends on its thickness. The purée must be firm and not liquid.

8 Serve on a dish with the meat and the purée side by side.

Notes:
– The cheese used in Greece and Turkey is usually *kasseri* but gruyere, or any relatively soft ('elastic' or melting) cheese may be used instead.
– A unique ingredient from Turkey, where it is used most widely in the south of the country, is capsicum or pepper paste (known as *biber salcasi*), a highly concentrated purée made from various types of cooked, peeled capsicums. This paste is included as an ingredient in most modern Turkish versions of this dish. Daphne's recipe was brought by the Greeks that came from Constantinople in the 1950s.

Stuffed chicken *(kotopoulo gemisto)*

Ingredients

1 whole chicken
250 g beef mince
1 large onion
2 tbsp pine nuts
2-3 tbsp currants
250 g chestnuts (boiled & peeled)
½ cup of olive oil
1 tbsp butter
1 cup risotto rice
1 tsp nutmeg (ground)
Salt/freshly ground black pepper

1 Take out the innards and cut off neck and tail parts, if any. Wash the chicken well.

2 Finely chop the onion and chestnuts.

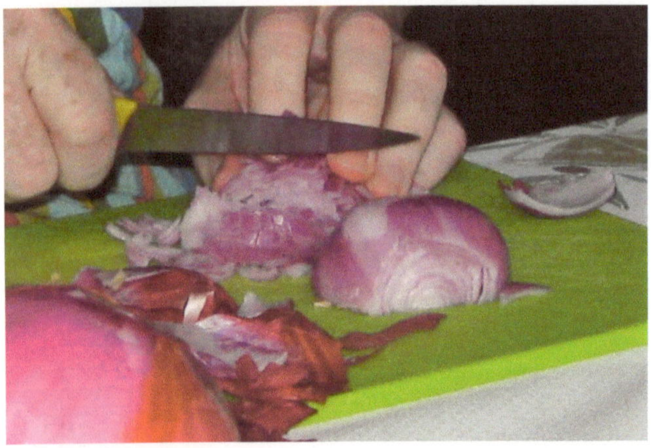

3 In a pan heat the oil and sauté the onions. Add the minced meat and fry.

4 Add the chestnuts, pine nuts and currants, mix it all well and then take off the heat.

5 Add the rice, salt, pepper and nutmeg, and then stuff the chicken with this mixture.

6 Put the butter into a bowl, melt it and season with salt and pepper. Brush this over the whole outside surface of the chicken.

7 Put the chicken into an oven dish and pack any remaining stuffing around the chicken, adding a cup of water. Note: the illustration on the next page shows a few chickens being done in this way.

8 Cover the stuffing with foil and bake in the oven at 180°C for about 1½ hours. During the baking check the stuffing and if necessary add more water. Brush more of the butterover the chicken. Towards end remove foil from stuffing and cook a little longer. The chicken must be sufficiently golden brown and the stuffing without liquid.

Stuffed baked lamb *(arnaki gemisto)*

Note: in Greece wherever possible it is traditional for the celebratory main meal on Easter Sunday to roast a whole lamb on a spit outdoors. But as an alternative, in Mytilini at least, Daphne prepares the lamb in this way.

Ingredients

3 kg lamb (breast and shoulder)
lamb's liver
500 g beef mince
2 cups risotto rice
1 cup dry white wine
½ cup olive oil
2 tbsp butter
1-2 onions
½ cup pine nuts
¾ cup currants or sultanas
Zest of an orange (optional)
2 tsp mixed spice (ground nutmeg, Cinnamon and cloves)
Salt/freshly ground black pepper

1 Boil the lamb's liver and then chop it up into small pieces.

2 Finely chop the onions. In a deep pan heat the oil and butter and sauté the onions until soft.

3 Add the mince and fry until brown.

4 Pour in the wine and cook until the liquid has evaporated.

5 Take the mince off the heat and add the chopped liver, rice, pine nuts, currants, zest, spices, salt and pepper. Mix all these ingredients very well.

6 Prepare the lamb: wipe it with a damp cloth externally only (skin side) and smear the inside with salt by hand.

7 Spoon the stuffing into the lamb; traditionally the lamb is stitched up with needle and thread so that the filling does not spill out during cooking. Alternatively, lay the lamb skin side down on some pieces of string, place the filling along the centre and fold the sides in so they overlap but not too tightly so the rice has room to expand. Tie it up with the string.

8 Season the outside with salt and pepper and place in an oven dish.

9 Into the dish pour 2½ cups of water and then bake in a preheated oven at 160°C for about 3 hours (each kilo of meat needs approximately one hour of cooking).

10 While it is cooking check on the meat to see if any more water is needed. With a brush baste the meat from time to time so that it does not dry out.

11 The lamb is ready when it is soft and juicy and has a crusty chestnut brown colour but not burnt.

Note: Daphne explains that for Greeks, Easter – and by Easter she means at least the entire Holy Week – is a very special period of devoutness and fasting.
"During that week almost everyone, even those who never go to church throughout the year, will light a candle on the day of the Crucifixion, will devoutly attend the Epitaph litany, will say *"Christos Anesti"* (Christ has risen) on the night of the Resurrection. On Easter Saturday, after midnight, every house will be filled with the aroma of the hot *'magiritsa'*, the soup prepared specially for the occasion.
"Of course, I am not suggesting that you have it on Easter Saturday midnight, but you can try it on a day when you are craving for soup. This rich soup has meat, vegetables, finished with egg and lemon sauce."
For a recipe see page 117.

Pastrami pie *(pastourmadopita)*

Ingredients

500 g fyllo pastry
600 g grated yellow cheese
3-4 fresh tomatoes
4-5 slices of pastrami
½ cup of tomato passata
½ cup of olive oil
A little vegetable oil to brush the oven dish

1 Preheat oven to 180°C.

2 Oil the oven dish and in it layer 6 sheets of *fyllo* pastry one by one, brushing each sheet with olive oil.

3 Sprinkle the grated cheese over the top.

4 Cut the pastrami into small pieces and sprinkle them over the cheese.

5 Cut the tomatoes into slices and place them on top.

6 Cover it all with the remaining sheets of *fyllo,* brushing the top of each one with oil except the last sheet.

7 With a sharp knife mark the portions with shallow cuts, while holding the top of the *fyllo* with the other hand to stop it from moving.

8 Mix the tomato passata with the olive oil and pour over the pie. Bake in the oven for about 40 minutes until light brown on top. Cut into portions and serve hot.

Aubergine Pie *(melitzanopita)*

Ingredients

5-6 aubergines
250 g minced beef
1 large onion
1 clove garlic
1 tin tomato passata (400 g)
Bunch of parsley
500 g fyllo pastry
200 g yellow cheese grated
1 egg
½ cup olive oil
Salt, pepper, nutmeg and pimento

1 Wash the aubergines and then cut them lengthwise into 1cm thick slices.

2 Lay the slices in an oiled oven dish. Oil the tops of the slices and bake in the oven until they are a golden colour and soft. This, as Daphne explains, is what is meant when Greeks say you decide "with the eye."

3 Finely slice the onion and the garlic, then sauté them in the olive oil. Add the minced beef, stirring until it starts to change colour. Add the tomato passata and spices and let it boil until the liquid is absorbed.

4 Leave both the aubergines and the mince to cool down.

5 On the worktop layer 4 sheets of *fyllo* pastry one by one, brushing each sheet with olive oil. On these put a layer of aubergine and over this sprinkle some salt and some grated cheese.

6 Over this lay another sheet of *fyllo* and then spread the mince mixture evenly on top of it. Sprinkle finely chopped parsley over the meat and cover it all with one more sheet of *fyllo*.

7 Mix the egg and the remaining grated cheese well, then lay it along a sheet of *fyllo* and roll it up into a rod-like form.

8 Put this *fyllo* 'rod' along one side of the layered base and using it as a core roll the whole pie up into a cylinder.

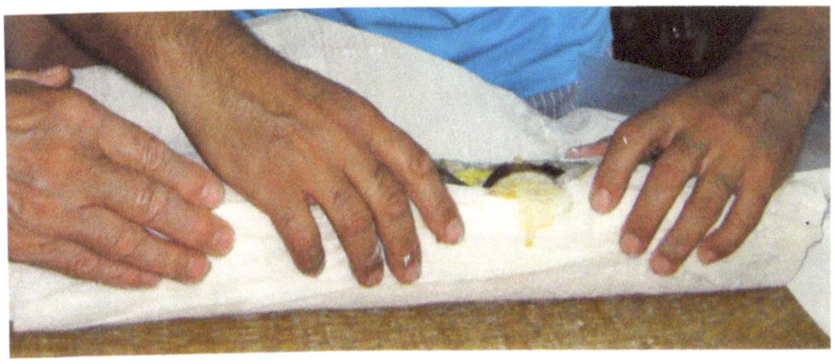

9 Carefully place the roll into an oiled oven-proof dish and with a sharp knife make shallow cuts in the top surface to mark the portions.

10 Bake in a preheated oven at 180°C for about 45 minutes or until the top is golden brown.

Smyrna meatballs *(soutzoukakia Smrneika)*

Notes:

– The recipe is believed to have originated in Smyrna, the old Greek city in Asia Minor that is called Izmir today.
–This is a very popular dish that with its rich sauce can make a good main course served with rice or mashed potatoes.
– Some people use parsley added to the meatballs, other use it as a garnish only. Daphne does not include it in her recipe, but I noticed that it seemed to be in the *souzoukakia* we made in the cooking class and wrote to her about this. The response I received from Votsala was "Daphne is very happy, because this is a confirmation of the Greek expression: 'He pops up like parsley,' used when somebody suddenly interrupts a discussion having an opinion about everything. So, parsley interferes everywhere, even in your soutzoukakia photo." Ultimately, the most important flavour is in the intensity of cumin, and according to some if there is no strong taste of this spice in the *soutzoukakia Smyrneika*, it loses all character and magic.

Ingredients

1 kg beef mince
1 egg
2-3 garlic cloves
2 tsp cumin
250 g bread crusts removed
1 cup olive oil
Salt/freshly ground black pepper
Flat leaf parsley, chopped (optional)

For the sauce:
2 tins (2 x 400 g) chopped tomatoes
1-2 tsp sugar
Salt/freshly ground black pepper
Flour for frying
Oil (sunflower) for frying

1 Put mince into a deep bowl. Soak the bread in water, then squeeze it well and add it to the mince.

2 Add salt, pepper, cumin, the egg, garlic (crushed or finely chopped) and half the olive oil to the mince.

3 Work the mixture very well by hand, then leave in the fridge for at least 30 minutes to allow the ingredients to blend.

4 Put oil into a frying pan and heat.

5 While this is happening take small amounts of the mixture and form into oblong (cigar or sausage) shapes (*soutzoukakia*).

6 In a dish with flour dust the *soutzoukakia*, shaking them well to get rid of excess flour. Fry in the hot oil for a short time on both sides. Turn with a spoon to avoid breaking them.

7 When fried pack the meatballs next to each other in a saucepan.

8 Put the tomato, salt, pepper and sugar into a bowl and mix well. Pour this sauce into the pan with the meatballs.

9 Add the other half of the olive oil and, if necessary, some water so that the meatballs are covered.

10 Cook on a low heat until the sauce has thickened – about 20 minutes.

Note: Daphne warns that one must not roll the *soutzoukakia* in the flour for too long before frying them b*ecause they absorb the flour and become* hard when fried.

Casserole with onions *(stifado)*

Note: *stifado* is traditionally made with wild rabbit but beef can be used as an alternative. There are many variations of this popular dish which should have a balance of sweet and sour: some with tomato and some without. Many use the sweet red wine mavrodaphne, or red wine vinegar rather than white wine; some use currants; and Daphne even suggests that adding prunes and carrots makes the *stifado* much tastier. The most important ingredient is onions — large quantities of pickling-sized onions — in Greece they are called *kokari*.

Ingredients

1 kg good quality stewing beef
1 tin (400 g) chopped tomato
1 kg small onion peeled
1 cup white wine
2 bay leaves
1 stick of cinnamon
3-4 grains of allspice
½-1 tsp sugar
½ cup of olive oil
Salt/freshly ground black pepper

1 Roughly dice the meat then lightly brown and seal it on all sides in hot oil.

2 Add the wine and cook slowly at a low temperature until the meat starts to soften. If necessary add some water.

3 Add the tomato, bay leaves, cinnamon, allspice, salt and pepper. Allow this to simmer for about an hour until the meat is cooked. Check from time to time and add boiling water if necessary.

4 Peel the baby onions, wash them and shallow fry (sauté) them in a little olive oil, until soft, not letting them burn.

5 Add the onions to the casserole and simmer further until the meat is meltingly tender and the sauce has thickened

Note: one can cook the *stifado* in the oven. After sautéing the meat and onions, the casserole can be baked in an oven dish at 180°C for about 2 to 2½ hours. It is important that this stew is slow cooked at a low temperature to achieve the melt-in-the-mouth quality. It can be made ahead of time and reheated — it tastes better after the herbs and spice have had time to blend.

Sausage-pepper stew *(spetzofai)*

Note: This is a traditional dish from Pelion, where it is known as *spentzofai*, and is served both in winter and summer as a spicy appetizer or main course. If spicy sausage is used take care with seasoning.

Ingredients

750 g pork sausages (ideally spicy)
750 g green peppers
750 g tomatoes
3 tbsp of olive oil
2 cloves of garlic
1 large bay leaf
1 heaped tbsp of dried oregano
1 cup dry red wine
Salt/freshly ground black pepper
1 chilli (optional)

1 Cut the sausages into about 10mm thick slices. Heat 1 tablespoon of olive oil in a nonstick frying pan and sauté the sausages over medium heat until browned all round. Remove sausage from pan and drain on paper towel.

2 Wash the peppers, cut them into slices lengthwise, and remove the seeds.

3 Peel and deseed the tomatoes then cut them into large pieces. Chop the garlic finely.

4 In the hot oil fry the peppers on a low heat until soft. Add the tomatoes, garlic, bay leaf and oregano and bring to a boil. Pour in the wine and mix in the sausage, salt and pepper. Lower the heat and simmer in a covered pan for about 30 minutes.

Baked meat with pasta *(youvetsi)*

Notes:

– This is typically tasty and tender Greek comfort food, made with chicken, lamb or beef and pasta, that for many islanders in particular is the perfect one for a family Sunday dinner. Traditionally served as a one-pot meal and baked in a round terracotta dish, from which it gets its name, it is nowadays most often done in the typical shallow aluminium dishes found everywhere. The only difficulty one might face with this dish is that it requires a certain amount of patience. It is not difficult to prepare but it needs time in the oven and is best cooked slowly.

– The most commonly used pasta is good quality orzo (from Italian for 'barley') made from durum wheat in the shape of a grain of rice. It is often about rice-sized, as well. Essentially identical is the very popular Greek *kritharáki*, ('little barley') and another traditional pasta used is *hlopitesi* (short-cut tagliatelle/fettuccine) or *hilopitaki* (Greek quadrettini). Any short-cut or small type of pasta can be used although orzo is regarded as the ideal one.

– Unlike Italian pasta a real, delicious *yiouvetsi* has its pasta overcooked and impregnated with the meat juices and the sweetness of fresh tomatoes.

Ingredients

800 g beef (or chicken or lamb)
2 medium-sized onions
1½ tins (400+200 g) chopped tomatoes
1 garlic clove
½ cup of olive oil
½ kg of orzo
1-2 bay leaves
1 tsp sugar
Salt/freshly ground black pepper
75 g of parmesan or similar cheese

1 Cut the meat into medium sized cubes and chop up the onions.

2 Heat oil in a deep pan and sauté the meat making sure it is browned evenly on all sides.

3 Add the onions and garlic and fry until they are light brown.

4 Cover with warm water and cook on a low heat until the meat is tender.

5 Add salt, pepper, sugar, bay leaves and chopped tomato and cook a little more on low heat.

6 Meanwhile boil the pasta in water for about 10 minutes, not letting it get too soft. Drain and rinse in a colander and place it into a deep oven-proof dish.

7 Add the meat and the sauce and one cup of water, then mix all well.

8 Place in a pre-heated oven at about 180°C for about 30 minutes.

9 Stir occasionally so that the pasta does not stick. If needed add some water, salt or pepper.

10 Serve immediately sprinkled with the grated cheese.

Greek pasta bake *(pastitsio)*

Note: *Pastitsio* takes its name from the Italian *pasticcio*, a large family of baked savory pies. The typical Greek version has a bottom layer of a tubular pasta, with cheese and/or egg as a binder; a middle layer of ground beef, or a mix of ground beef and ground pork with tomato; and a top layer that is a flour-based béchamel. *Pastitsio* is a traditional dish, and is often served as a main course, with a salad.

Ingredients

500 g penne (or other tubular pasta)
½ cup olive oil
500-750 g minced meat (beef)
2 large onions
1 garlic clove
1-2 tbsp finely chopped parsley
½ tsp ground allspice
½ tsp cinnamon
1-2 bay leaves
1½ tins (400+200 g) chopped tomatoes
1-2 tsp sugar
Salt/freshly ground black pepper

For the bechamel sauce:

4-5 tbsp butter
4 tbsp flour
1 litre warm milk
1 cup grated yellow cheese
A pinch of nutmeg
1 egg
Salt/freshly ground black pepper

1 Pasta: in a large pan bring salted water to the boil. Add the pasta and cook until al dente, taking care not to over-cook as the pasta will cook further in the oven. Drain well, put into to a bowl and leave to cool slightly.

For the meat sauce:

2 Finely chop both the onions and garlic.

3 Heat the oil in a saucepan, add the onions and garlic, and sauté lightly until soft.

4 Add the mince and stir continuously until the meat is browned.

5 Then add parsley, salt, pepper, sugar, nutmeg, bay leaves and chopped tomatoes.

6 Cook on a low heat for about half an hour until the liquid has evaporated.

For the béchamel:

7 in a medium sized pan melt the butter then add the flour. Using a whisk stir until it has taken on a light brown colour.

8 Gradually add milk and keep on stirring.

9 When the sauce has thickened take it off the heat. Daphne says she likes the sauce to be not too thick!

10 After it has cooled a little add the egg, salt, pepper, nutmeg and grated cheese while stirring continuously.

Assemble the pastitsio:

11 Use some melted butter to grease a deep oven dish. Place the pasta in a layer at the bottom. Pour some of the bechamel sauce on it and mix.

12 Spread the mince mixture over the pasta, and then over the top of this a layer of béchamel sauce.

13 Bake in a preheated oven at 180°C for about an hour until golden brown.

Note:
Some people add 100-200 ml of red wine to the meat mixture.

Skewerless kebab *(yiaourtlou)*

Note: there are two basic forms of pita or pitta — a family of yeast-leavened round flatbreads baked from wheat flour, common in the Mediterranean, Middle East, and neighbouring areas — firstly, a widely known version with an interior pocket, also known as Arabic bread; secondly, a pocketless version such as the Greek pita, used to wrap *souvlaki*.

Ingredients

1 kg mince meat (all beef or half lamb)
2 onions & 1 garlic clove
250 g bread (without crusts)
1 egg
½ cup olive oil
1 tsp coriander powder (optional)
Salt/freshly ground black pepper
400 g Greek yoghurt
Pittas ideal the souvlaki type
Parsley for garnish

For the sauce:
2 tins (2x400 g) chopped tomatoes
1 large onion
1-2 tsp sugar
2 tbsp olive oil
Salt/freshly ground black pepper

1 Place the mince in a deep bowl.

2 Soak the bread and squeeze out the water very well.

3 Chop up the onion and add the crushed garlic.

4 Add the bread, onion, garlic, coriander, egg, salt, pepper and oil to the mince and mix it all very well by hand. Leave to rest in the fridge for 30 minutes for the ingredients to blend.

5 Meanwhile, for the sauce finely chop the onion and then sauté in heated oil until soft and light brown.

6 Add tomato, sugar, salt and pepper and cook over medium heat until it thickens.

7 Take the mince mixture from the fridge and form small amounts into big oblong, cigar-like shapes. Place them next to each other in an oiled oven dish. Bake in preheat oven at 180°C for about 45 minutes.

8 Toast the pittas and then cut into pieces. On each piece put some yogurt and *yiaourtlou* on top. Finally pour some sauce over it and garnish with parsley. As Daphne says, it is delicious to eat the crispy pittas, the kebabs and the sauce hot but the yogurt cool, so serve immediately.

Stuffed onions *(kremidodolmades)*

Note: these onions are usually regarded as a *meze* on the island of Lesvos where they are also called *sougania.*

Ingredients

300 g beef mince
7-8 large onions or banana shallots
½-¾ cup risotto rice
¾ cup olive oil
½ bunch parsley
1 teaspoon cumin
Salt/freshly ground black pepper

For the egg-lemon sauce:
2 eggs
1 lemon
1 tbsp cornflour
Salt/freshly ground black pepper

1 Boil water in a saucepan.

2 Peel the onions and make a cut lengthwise without cutting right through.

3 Place the onions in the heated water and boil over a low heat until they become soft and open.

4 Take the onions out of the water with a perforated spoon and put onto absorbent paper; leave to cool. Then carefully separate the layers and put the larger ones to the side.

5 Finely chop the smallest onion layers and the parsley. In a deep bowl mix the mince, rice, chopped parsley and onion, oil, cumin, salt and pepper.

6 Using a large teaspoon spoon fill the centres of the onion shells with the mixture and then wrap them tightly.

7 In an oiled saucepan carefully pack the stuffed onions, slit side down, closely next to each other, and then covered with water.

8 Pour the rest of the oil over the onions and cover with a plate. Cook over medium heat for about 30 minutes.

When almost cooked prepare the egg-lemon sauce:

9 Squeeze the lemon removing any pips.

10 In a deep bowl beat the two eggs well. Beating continuously add the lemon juice, a little salt and pepper. Then add the corn flour which has been diluted in a little cold water.

11 Take a little of the hot liquid from the cooking onions and gradually pour this into the egg-lemon, stirring continuously.

12 Remove the onions from the heat and pour in the egg-lemon sauce, shaking the pan to ensure that sauce mixes in well.

13 Leave the pan to stand for a while so that the sauce is smooth and thick.

Pork with celery *(hirino me selino)*

Notes:
– This delicate dish is served with egg-lemon sauce.
– Keep in mind that the celery in Greece, which comes in thin bunches of slender greenery, is completely different from that in the west. So, the appearance of the dish is rather different.
– Daphne points out the chicken and lamb can be used in place of pork in the recipe.

Ingredients

1 kg lean, boneless pork
1 large onion
½-¾ cup olive oil
1-1½ kg celery
Salt/freshly ground black pepper

For the egg-lemon sauce:
2 eggs
1-2 lemons
1 tbsp cornflour
Salt/freshly ground black pepper

1 Cut the meat into pieces and finely chop the onion.

2 Heat the oil in a saucepan. Add the meat and cook, turning it with a fork until light brown on all sides.

3 Remove the meat with a slotted spoon, and lightly fry the onion in the same pan.

4 Put the meat back into the saucepan with the onion and add 2-3 cups of water. Cook over low heat for around an hour.

5 When the meat has become sufficiently tender, season with salt and pepper. While the meat is cooking…

6 Wash and clean the celery, then cut into large pieces removing the very hard pieces and fibres.

7 Fill a large saucepan with water and add the celery. Bring to the boil two or three times throw away the water each time and use new water.

8 When the celery has softened, strain it. Put the celery into the saucepan with the meat, add some water. Cook for a further 10-15 minutes until the celery is very tender.

9 When the dish is almost cooked prepare the egg-lemon sauce all as described on pages 102 and 103.

10 Take the meat and celery off the heat and pour in the egg-lemon sauce, shaking the saucepan in order to ensure that the sauce mixes in well everywhere.

11 Leave it to stand for a while until the sauce is smooth and thick.

Meat with quinces *(kydonato)*

Notes:
– This was one of the formal dishes in Daphne's home.
– According to her the aroma of the dish is given by the quinces, so the meat is cooked simply without wine, bay leaf and spices. The small tomato is just to give the dish a pinkish colour.

Ingredients
1 kg beef
¾ cup olive oil
4-5 medium quinces
1 onion
1 tomato
2 teaspoons sugar
1 tbsp butter
Salt/freshly ground black pepper

1 Cut the meat into pieces and finely chop the onion.

2 Heat oil in a saucepan, then put in the meat and fry on all sides, stirring with a fork. As soon as the meat has browned, take it out, put in the onion and sauté lightly.

3 Return the meat to the pan again, add a little water and cook over a low heat. Grate the tomato and add it to the meat.

4 Season with salt and pepper and add half a teaspoon of sugar. Allow the meat to cook until tender.

5 In the meantime cut the quinces in half, and then each half into 3 or 4 slices lengthways in half-moon shapes. Peel and core the pieces.

6 In a non-stick pan heat up the butter and then lightly sauté the quinces. While in the pan sprinkle the remaining sugar over them and allow it to caramelize a little. Pouring a little brandy over the top gives the dish a lovely aroma.

7 Pour the sauce from the quinces into the casserole, lower the heat and cook until the sauce has thickened slightly. Place the quinces on top of the meat and turn the heat off.

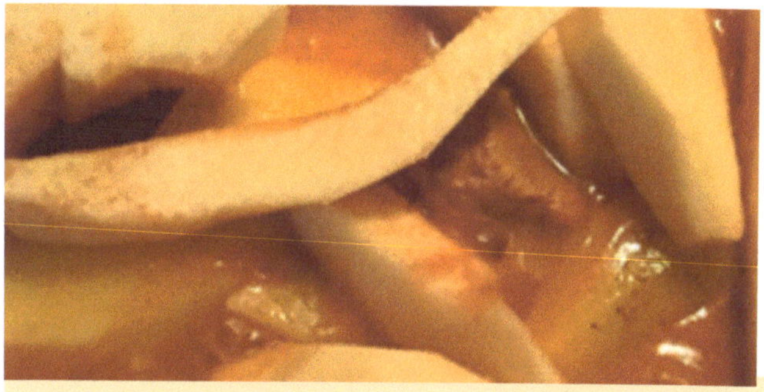

Note: This same casserole can be found in many variations all over Greece and is sometimes made with lamb or boned pork.

Pork with prunes *(hirino me damaskina)*

Ingredients

2 kg pork
4 oranges
1 cup brandy
2 tbsp butter
2 tbsp olive oil
100 g prunes (dried no stones)
100 g apricots (dried)
100 g boiled chestnuts
2 tbsp mustard
1 tbsp honey
Salt/freshly ground black pepper

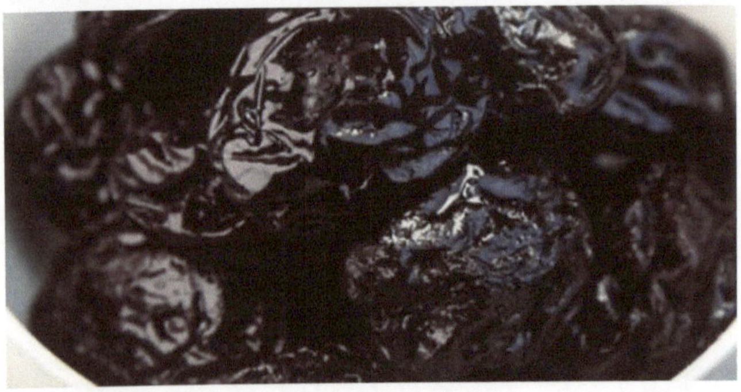

1 Heat the oil and butter in a large saucepan. When sufficiently hot fry the meat on all sides until light brown and a crust has formed.

2 Pour brandy over the meat — keep 2 tbsp for the sauce.

3 Squeeze the oranges and set aside 2 tbsp for the sauce.

4 Cut the prunes, apricots and chestnuts in half.

5 Take the meat out of the saucepan and put it into an oven dish with its gravy.

6 Pour the orange juice over the meat and add the prunes, apricots and chestnuts to the dish.

7 Season the meat with salt and pepper.

8 Blend the honey and mustard together with the reserved brandy and orange juice in a food processor. Brush half the mixture over the meat.

9 Cook the meat in a preheated oven at 160ºC for about 2 hours.

10 Halfway through the cooking brush the meat with the other half of the mixture. If necessary add a little more orange juice.

11 Towards the end of cooking increase the oven temperature to 200ºC for about 20-30 minutes.

12 Daphne suggests the pork can be served with potatoes that have been baked whole in foil

Ottoman chicken

Ingredients
6 chicken breast fillets
16 dried apricots
2 tbsp butter
1 cup brandy
1½ cups soft yellow cheese grated
mild curry powder
250 ml fresh cream
Salt/freshly ground black pepper

1 Cut the apricots in half and put then to soak in the brandy for at least 30 minutes.

2 Wash the chicken and cut it into large cubes.

3 In a heated pan melt the butter and fry the chicken stirring constantly until it takes on a brown colour.

4 Add the apricots together with the brandy and stir until the fruit is soft.

5 Put the chicken and fruit into a baking dish, add the cheese, cream, curry, salt and pepper and mix well.

6 Bake in a preheated oven at 180°C for approximately 40 minutes.

7 Serve with rice.

Moussaka

Note: this is without doubt the best-known Greek dish and is served at every taverna frequented by tourists. Unfortunately, it is usually too oily. As Daphne says: "There are several versions of *moussaka* in Greece. You easily find it in every touristic place but never in restaurants where locals go. The reason is that for Greeks the only good *moussaka* is the one their mum makes for them!" In most tavernas they always add potatoes — a traditional version in Macedonia does contain a thin layer of potato that has been fried first — but Daphne adds: "my mother-in-law used to say that this was *moussaka* for the poor people. I have to tell you that our version is also tasty the next day. The potatoes next day do not taste so good!"

Ingredients

5 large aubergines
½-¾ kg minced beef
2 large onions
1 garlic clove (optional)
1-2 tbsp chopped parsley
½ tsp ground allspice
1-2 bay leaves
1½ tins (400+200 g) chopped tomatoes
1-2 tsp of sugar
1 cup olive oil
1 cup wine (optional)
Salt/freshly ground black pepper

Béchamel sauce:

4-5 tbsp butter
4 tbsp plain flour
1 litre lukewarm milk
1 egg
1 cup yellow grated cheese
½-1 tsp nutmeg
Salt/freshly ground black pepper

1 Wash and dry the aubergines. Cut off the stems and cut lengthwise into slices about 6mm thick.

2 Arrange the aubergine slices in an oiled baking dish. Salt lightly and brush with oil. Bake them in a preheated oven at 180°C until soft.

Meanwhile prepare the meat sauce:

3 Finely chop the onions and the parsley. Sauté in hot oil, stirring until transparent.

4 Add the minced meat and stir continuously until the mince turns brown.

5 Add wine, tomatoes, parsley, salt, pepper, allspice, bay leaves and sugar. Mix well, lower the heat and allow to simmer for about ½ hour, until most of the liquid has evaporated.

Time to prepare the bechamel sauce:

6 In a medium-sized saucepan melt the butter and add the flour. Stir constantly using an egg-whisk, until the flour turns golden brown.

7 Add the milk, gradually stirring constantly. When the sauce thickens take it off the heat.

8 Let it cool down and then stir in cheese, egg, salt, pepper and nutmeg.

9 In a greased baking dish, layer the aubergines and minced meat. Pour the bechamel sauce over the top.

10 Bake in a preheated oven at 180°C for at least 1 hour until the surface turns golden brown and crusty.

Notes:

– Daphne explains that Greeks do not traditionally bake the aubergine in the oven as she does, but fry them instead. If you use this method it is best to first sprinkle the slices of aubergine with salt and set them aside in a colander for about an hour to allow them to 'sweat'. After frying drain the excess oil using absorbent kitchen paper towel.

– Daphne suggests that if one has lumps in the bechamel sauce, one should add more butter and stir well.

– Because more and more guests at the hotel are vegetarian she has created a suitable Moussaka as follows:

1 In a baking dish arrange slices of aubergine, zucchini and green peppers, that have all been pre-baked in the oven as for the main recipe.

2 Add tomato sauce and crumbled feta or other grated cheese and repeat once again all the layers — vegetables, tomato sauce and cheese.

3 Cover with bechamel sauce and bake as for the main recipe.

Baked burger with potatoes
(biftekia sto fourno)

Ingredients

1 kg beef mince
2 medium onions
250 g bread without crusts
1 egg
2 tbsp oregano
½ cup olive oil
3-4 large potatoes
1 lemon
Salt/freshly ground black pepper

1 Soak bread in water and then squeeze it out well. Chop up the onions.

2 Put the mince into a bowl and add the bread, onions, egg, salt, pepper, half of the oregano, and half of the oil. Mix well by hand and then allow to rest for 30 minutes.

3 Peel, wash and cut the potatoes into medium sized pieces.

4 Divide the mince into equal portions and pat each into a flat round shape about the size of a flat egg.

5 Put the burgers into a lightly oiled oven dish leaving some space between them.

6 Put the potatoes into a bowl and season with salt and pepper. Add the remaining oil and oregano and mix well.

7 Fit the potatoes between the burgers in the oven dish.

8 Squeeze the lemon and pour the juice as well as a cup of water over it all.

9 Bake in a preheated oven at 180°C for about an hour.

Note: Some people believe that these ‘burgers’ are best when made with tender and lean minced lamb. They believe they are more succulent, and the flavour is better. These burgers can, of course be grilled or barbecued.

Stuffed zucchini *(kolokithakia gemista)*

Ingredients

8-10 zucchini (medium sized)
300 g beef mince
1 large onion
1 handful mint (fresh or dried)
1 handful dill (fresh or dried)
½ cup risotto rice
½ cup olive oil
Salt/freshly ground black pepper

For the egg-lemon sauce:
2 eggs
1 lemon
1 tbsp cornflour
Salt/freshly ground black pepper

1 Wash the zucchini and cut off the stem ends.

2 Scoop out the centre with an apple corer or a long-handled teaspoon, and set aside half of the pulp to use in the filling. Throw away the other half or keep it to use for an omelette. Be careful not to get too close to the skin of the zucchini.

3 Chop up the onion and mix with the scooped pulp. Finely chop the mint and dill.

4 In a bowl mix the mince well with all the other ingredients and then stuff the zucchini with this.

5 Arrange them side by side in a deep pan. Choose the size of pan in order to fit one or two layers of the zucchini.

6 Cover with water, add some salt, and cook on medium heat until the zucchini are soft when tested with a fork.

7 When almost cooked prepare the egg-lemon sauce all as described on page 84.

8 Take the zucchini off the heat and pour in the egg-lemon sauce, shaking the saucepan in order to ensure that the sauce mixes in well everywhere.

7 Leave it to stand for a while until the sauce is smooth and thick.

Meat pie with leeks *(kreatopita me prassa)*

Ingredients

½ kg coarse mince (½ beef & ½ pork)
½ cup olive oil
3-4 fresh spring onions
1 onion
3-4 leeks (white part only)
½ bunch parsley
½ bunch dill
250 g medium hard cheese
2 eggs
Salt/freshly ground black pepper

For the dough:
1 cup warm water
4 tbsp olive oil
2 tbsp ouzo (or rum, beer or just water)
4-4½ cups flour
Salt

1 Finely chop the spring onions, onion, leeks, parsley and dill.

2 In a wide pan heat the oil. Add the mince and fry until brown.

3 Take the mince out when ready and in the same pan…

4 Put in all the onions and the leeks and stir till soft then…

5 Add the mince back into the pan, season with salt and pepper, and cook for about 5 minutes. Take off the heat, add parsley and dill then allow to cool.

Meanwhile prepare the dough:

6 In a bowl mix the water, oil, ouzo and salt. Gradually add the flour until there is a soft, malleable dough.

7 Allow the dough to rest for a short time. Divide it into two pieces, one a little larger than the other. Lightly flour a surface and roll out both pieces.

8 Oil an oven dish and lay down the larger piece of dough so that it covers the bottom and overhangs the sides.

9 Place the filling in the dish and turn the overhanging side pieces of dough inwards. Cover the pie with the second piece of dough.

10 Score the top and bake in a preheated oven at 180°C for about 45-50 minutes until golden brown.

Note: Daphne says that if one does not want to make the pastry, one can use ready-made *fyllo* all as described in the cheese pie recipe on page 45.

Wild rabbit in wine *(kouneli sto krassi)*

Notes:

- Wild rabbit is highly valued as a delicious meat throughout Europe but is sadly underrated in the UK where it is usually available from game butchers either whole or ready jointed. A lean meat with excellent meat to bone ratio, it is enjoying a renaissance with many celebrity chefs and restaurants putting it back on their menus.
- It has a mild gamey almost chicken-like flavour and can be tender and delicious as an alternative to farmed meat. It is a sustainable meat, has a higher protein content than beef or chicken, and is lower in calories. The flavour can be enhanced by hanging or diluted by soaking the meat in water with added vinegar for two or three hours before cooking.
- In Greece the rabbit meat is almost always marinated in a solution of water and vinegar. This process also 'cleans' the meat of any blood residue. Wild rabbit can be cooked in a variety of ways and is excellent in stews, casseroles, pies and goulashes. Although the meat tends to be dryer, rabbit can be used in many dishes as an alternative to chicken.

Ingredients

1 rabbit in serving size pieces
2 onions
¾ cup olive oil
2 cups white wine
1 heaped tsp of oregano dried
Salt/freshly ground black pepper
Bay leaf (optional)

1 Rinse the rabbit pieces and put them in a bowl with the bay leaf, sprinkle vinegar over all, and let them marinade for at least 2 hours or in the fridge overnight.

2 Chop the onions.

3 Heat the oil in a deep pan, pat the rabbit pieces dry and fry them lightly on all sides.

4 Add the onion and fry until light brown. Then add the wine, salt, pepper and oregano.

5 Cover with water and simmer until the rabbit is tender and the sauce has thickened.

6 Serve with rice or boiled potatoes.

Kleftiko 1

For a variation of this recipe see Appendix 1.

Notes:

– Daphne explains that this is one of the truly traditional rustic dishes of Greece, known because of its simple, but at the same time very complicated, way of baking. The name *kleftiko* comes from the robbers (*kleftes*) — who eventually became successful freedom fighters — living on the mountains during the Ottoman occupation. They were notorious for stealing sheep and roasting the animal in its skin, buried in a sealed underground pit so that neither the aroma nor the smoke from the fire would be detected.

– So, *kleftiko*, literally meaning "in the style of the ***klephts***", is basically lamb slow-baked on the bone. Nowadays it is usually baked sealed, wrapped in a tight parchment paper parcel to keep all the juices and flavours inside. Often cooked in one big parcel together with various vegetables, it seems better to prepare it in separate individual packets that make it easy to serve.

– Many versions can be found today throughout Greece and the recipe that follows is Daphne's own. She reports that she recently cooked it for friends, and they thought it was delicious! The quantity of meat and vegetables give 6-8 portions (packets/pouches).

– Leg of lamb, boneless if individual portions are being made, is most commonly used. However, lamb fillets and lamb shanks also work well in the separate packets described in this recipe.

Ingredients (to serve about 6-8)

800-1,000 g lamb leg
200 g feta cheese
2-3 peppers (red, yellow and green)
1-2 carrots
1-2 potatoes
1-2 zucchini
1 large onion
3-4 cloves garlic
½ cup parsley
1 handful oregano
1 handful dried or fresh mint
½ cup olive oil
Salt/freshly ground black pepper
Greaseproof paper & some string

1 Cut the meat into the required number of serving portions or into large cubes.

2 Cut the peppers, carrots, potatoes and zucchini into cubes.

3 Slice the onions and garlic. Finely chop the parsley.

4 In a large frying pan heat the oil and then lightly fry the meat.

5 Take out the sautéed meat and in the same oil lightly fry the onion and garlic. Take them out and then in the same pan fry the peppers, carrots, potatoes and zucchini.

6 Take out the vegetables and set them aside with the onion and garlic.

7 Put the meat back in the pan, add some water and let it boil until tender.

8 When the meat is ready take it off the heat and add parsley, oregano, and mint, season with salt and pepper and mix well.

9 Cut the greaseproof/parchment paper into about 30+ cm square, so that each piece can hold a serving of meat, and vegetables.

10 Place the serving of meat and vegetables plus some feta in the centre of the paper, gather together the edges and form a pouch, then tie with string.

11 Put the pouches into an oven dish and bake in a preheated oven at 180°C for about an hour.

Note: each pouch is a meal in itself and does not normally require any accompaniment.

Aubergine 'little shoes'
(papoutsakia)

Notes:
– For the vegetarian version of this dish see page 63.
–In Greece these are invariably served as a main course and as they are rather rich half an aubergine per person may be sufficient.
– This classic dish gets the odd name from its final appearance.

Ingredients *(serves 2-4)*

2 large (or 3 medium) aubergines
1-2 onions
200-250 g minced beef
½ tin (200 g) chopped tomatoes or 2 fresh tomatoes
Olive oil
1 bay leaf
1 garlic clove
1 tbsp chopped parsley
½ cup red wine
½ tsp ground cinnamon
1 tsp sugar
Salt/freshly ground black pepper

For the bechamel sauce
50 g butter
½ cup flour
1½ cups (180 g) milk
1 egg
A little freshly ground nutmeg
Salt/freshly ground black pepper

1 Wash and dry the aubergines – do not cut off the stems. Cut them in half lengthways. Scoop some of the pulp out from the middle and set aside.

2 Oil an oven dish as well as coating the aubergines all over.

3 Place them in the dish face down and bake at 180°C for 30 minutes.

Meanwhile prepare the mince filling

4 Finely chop the onions, garlic and parsley.

5 In a saucepan heat olive oil and sauté the onions and garlic until soft, then add the mincemeat and the aubergine pulp stirring constantly until it turns light brown.

6 Add the wine, tomatoes, parsley, salt, pepper, cinnamon, bay leaf and sugar. Lower the heat and allow to simmer for 30 minutes until most of the liquid has gone.

Do not forget to take the aubergines out of the oven!! Now prepare the bechamel sauce

7 In a saucepan melt the butter and add the flour stirring constantly with a whisk until the flour turns brown.

8 Add the milk gradually continuing to stir constantly. When the sauce thickens take it off the heat.

9 When it has cooled down stir in the egg, nutmeg, salt and pepper.

10 Arrange the aubergines side by side in a baking dish and fill them with the meat mixture. Cover the tops with the thick bechamel. Some people like to add a little grated cheese on top.

11 Bake in a preheated oven at 180ºC for about 45-60 minutes, until they are a golden brown

Traditional Easter soup *(magiritsa)*

Note: this is a modified version of the soup traditionally made with lamb intestines. See also note on page…

Ingredients *(serves 4)*

½ kg lamb
1 lamb's liver (optional)
6-7 spring onions
2 lettuces
1 bunch dill
1 cup risotto rice
1 cup olive oil
Salt/freshly ground black pepper
For the egg-lemon sauce
2 eggs
Juice of 1-2 lemons
1 tbsp cornflour
Salt/pepper

1 Put the meat in a saucepan and cover with water and bring to the boil. When boiled put the broth from the meat aside and cut up the meat into small pieces.

2 Do the same with the liver.

3 Finely chop the spring onions, lettuce and dill.

4 Put the reserved broth into a saucepan and add the chopped ingredients, season with salt and pepper. If needed add water so that all the ingredients are covered. Cook on a medium heat for about 30 minutes.

5 Add the rice and oil and continue to cook for about 15 minutes until the rice is done.

Meanwhile prepare the egg-lemon sauce:

6 *In a bowl beat the eggs well and add the lemon juice, as well as a little salt and pepper beating continuously.*

7 *Add the cornflower which has been diluted in a little cold water.*

8 *Take a little of the hot soup from the saucepan and gradually pour this into the egg-lemon mixture stirring continuously.*

9 *Take the soup off the heat and pour in the egg-lemon sauce while stirring vigorously.*

10 *Return to a very gentle heat for a few minutes while still stirring so all the ingredients blend well.*

Rice with leftover meat *(atzem pilaf)*

Notes:
– A popular dish and widely used in Greece.
– Daphne says that during her childhood they would only have meat on a Sunday, so every Monday her mother would use all the meat leftover from the previous day's lunch.
– She writes: "Perhaps my childhood memories have now been distorted by time, but I believe that this simple dish is worth trying when there is some left-over meat. *Atzem* rice is always white in my mind's eye." It seems that when there was also tomato sauce left over her mother would not use rice, but rather pasta baked in the oven.

Ingredients

¾ kg meat approximately
3 tbsp butter
2 cups rice
1 onion
1 apple
Salt/freshly ground black pepper

1 Cut the meat into small pieces.

2 Put the meat into a pan with some water, and season with a little salt and pepper and let it cook for a while.

3 Finely chop the onion and apple, and then sauté them lightly in oil.

4 Add them to the meat, and then add the rice with about 3 cups of hot water stirring it all well.

5 Cook until the rice is done. Remove from the heat cover with a towel and leave for 10 minutes. Melt the butter and pour this over the food.

Fish and seafood *(psaria kai thalassina)*

In his book *Courtesans and Fishcakes*, James Davidson's concern is with ancient appetites in classical Athens. Fish, he makes clear, loomed large: it was the gourmet food and ancient Greek writer wrote more about fish than any other food. He writes: "The Greeks were fond of fish. Fondness, on second thoughts, is rather too moderate a word for such a passion. What the literature of pleasure manifests, time and time again, is something rather more intense, a craving, a maddening addiction, an indecent obsession".

Nothing much has changed and the appetite for fish remains as strong today even if it is only an occasional portion. Although surrounded by water Greeks are not first and foremost seafarers but people of the land — farmers and shepherds preoccupied with their olives, vines, fields and flocks. Fish can be very expensive, though there are inexpensive ones such as sardines, anchovies and smelt available year-round, and these are just as tasty as the expensive ones. Other fish and seafood that is used quite commonly includes squid, cuttlefish, octopus, swordfish, tuna, red mullet, seabream, seabass and cod.

In the Aegean, as everywhere else it seems, intensive commercial fishing is causing the fish stock to deplete year by year. Nowadays even some of the small traditional fishing boats in these parts are fitted not only with powerful engines, but also sophisticated equipment such as echo-location devices.

Octopus in wine *(ktapodi krasato)*

Notes:
– Octopus, fresh or frozen, always needs a good rinsing because there is sand, especially in its hood.
– In Greece it is cooked in a number of ways but mostly with wine, which is thought to add a soothing element and make the octopus more digestible. Also, salt is never added to fresh octopus from the Aegean. However, the frozen version from the Atlantic may need some.

Ingredients
1 octopus, approx. 1½ kg
1 large onion
¾-1 cup olive oil
1½ cups of red wine
2 bay leaves
½ cup vinegar (optional)
10 black peppercorns
5 granules of allspice

1 Wash the octopus very well and rinse under running water. Cut it into 3-4 cm pieces.

2 Place a shallow saucepan onto the heat. When hot put in the octopus without any water and wait until its liquid comes out. Keep turning the pieces with a wooden spoon until all the liquid has evaporated.

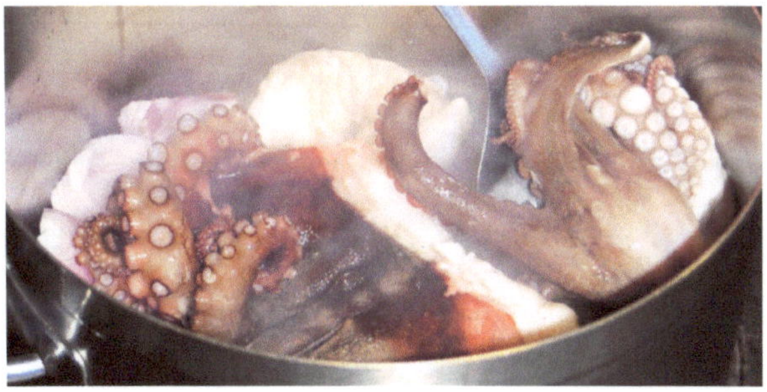

3 Add onion cut into two, wine, bay leaves, pepper and allspice. Lower the heat to medium and cover the pan. Cook until the liquid is almost absorbed, and the octopus becomes soft.

4 Add the oil and vinegar, then cook for another 10-15 minutes without cover on a high heat.

5 Serve with its sauce and some oregano (optional) on the top.

Stuffed squid *(kalamarakia gemista)*

Ingredients

10 medium-sized squid
½ cup risotto rice
1 small ripe tomato
½ bunch dill
½ bunch parsley
1 large onion
¾ cup olive oil
2-3 handfuls pine nuts
2-3 handfuls currants
1 tbsp orange zest finely chopped
½ cup dry white wine
Salt/freshly ground black pepper

1 Clean the squid removing bone and the small ink bag. Remove the tentacles and chop them up.

3 Heat half the oil in a non-stick pan and fry the onions lightly on a low heat. When ready add the chopped tentacles and cook until soft.

4 Add the rice, currants, pine nuts, parsley, dill, salt, pepper and orange zest. Stir well. Pour in the wine and tomato and cook for 5-8 minutes.

5 Remove from the heat and stuff the squid about ¾ full to allow room for the rice to expand.

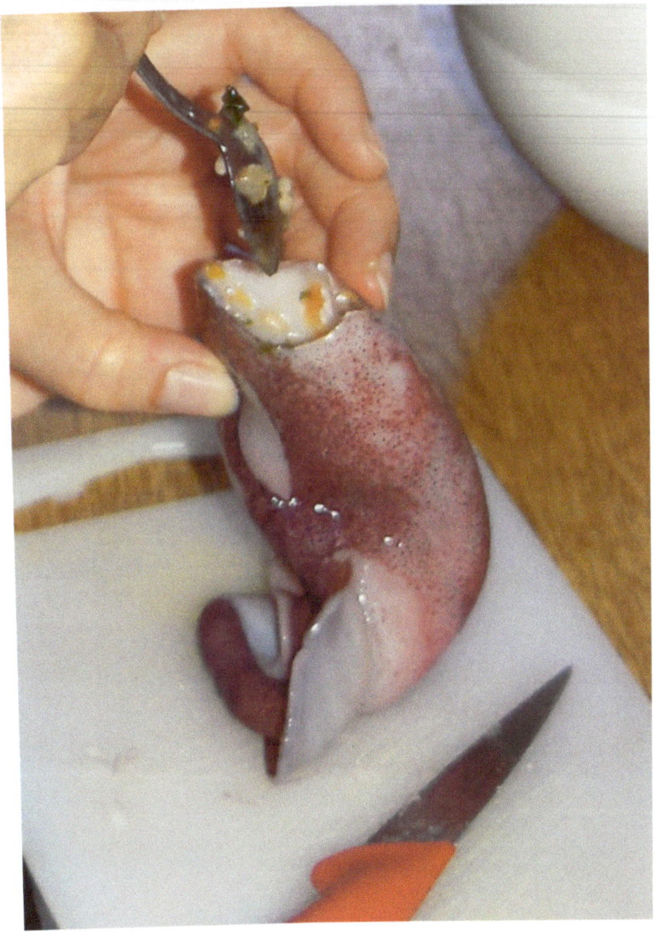

6 Seal the ends with a toothpick and place in a wide pan.

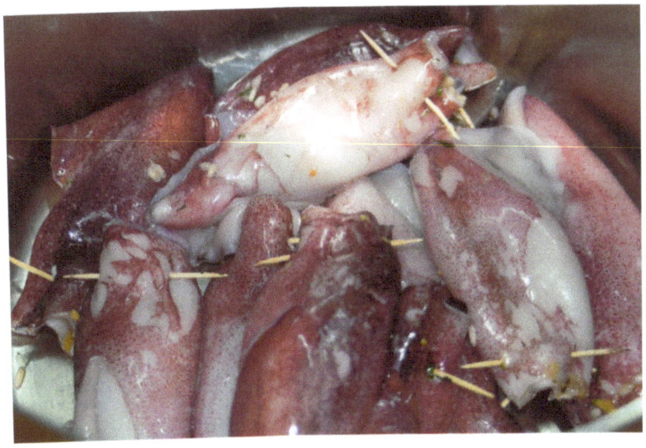

7 Pour in the rest of the oil, add salt and 1½ cups of water, and simmer until the squid is soft and the sauce has thickened. If necessary add water during the cooking.

8 Remove the toothpicks carefully before serving. Strain the sauce and pour it over the squid.

Notes:
– Daphne says that on Lesvos they always use orange zest, but this is not the case in other parts of Greece. So, if the taste or aroma of orange does not appeal to one it can be omitted.
– Also, if one does not like currants, or does not have any, a teaspoon of sugar can be added instead.
– Tradition says one should sew up the *kalamari* with thread using a thick needle. However, nowadays Daphne uses toothpicks.

Baked fish with ouzo *(psari me ouzo)*

Notes:
Daphne gives a variation of this dish that is liked by her son. For this, she adds to the ingredients below thinly sliced potatoes, carrots and different coloured peppers (in addition to those below). First she lays out the potatoes seasoned with salt and pepper. After this she continues with layers of zucchini and the other vegetables (except the tomatoes), adding a drop more oil.
She points out that one may use frozen fish and there is no need to defrost it first.
Lastly, in the main recipe, if there are no fresh tomatoes available one may use a tin of chopped tomatoes instead.

Ingredients:
1 kg sardines or other fish fillets
3 large ripe tomatoes
½ kg zucchini
1 bunch parsley
2-3 garlic cloves
1 onion
¾ cup olive oil
½ cup ouzo or white wine
Salt/freshly ground black pepper
Some oregano

1 Wash the zucchini and cut it into 1 cm thick slices. Finely chop the parsley.

2 Brush an oven dish with half the oil.

3 Lay the zucchini slices in the dish, and then salt them.

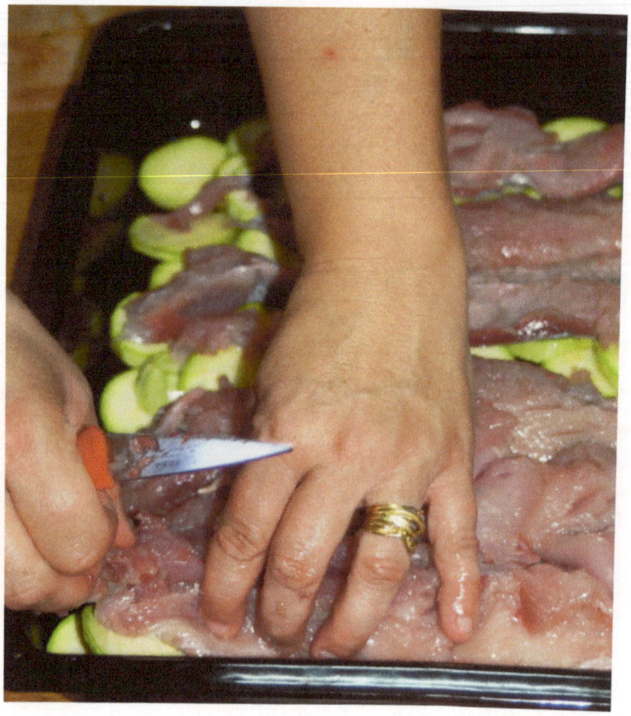

4 Next place the fish over the zucchini.

5 Cut the tomatoes, onion and garlic into slices and place in a layer over the fish.

6 Pour the ouzo (or wine) over the tomatoes, add the salt, pepper and oregano. If one wishes a few more slices of zucchini can be put on top and then sprinkle parsley over it all.

7 Add the remaining oil and bake in the oven at 180°C for about 45 minutes.

Shrimp saganaki *(garides saganaki)*

Ingredients (serves 3-4 as a side dish)

250 g shrimps peeled
1 onion
1 garlic clove
1 tomato or ½ tin chopped tomato
½ tsp sugar
70 g feta cheese
½ bunch parsley
¼ cup olive oil
Salt/freshly ground black pepper

1 Finely chop the onion, garlic, tomato, and parsley. Crumble the feta.

2 Heat the oil in a pan and then lightly fry the onion and garlic until soft.

3 Add the tomato, sugar, salt, and pepper. Allow the sauce to boil and thicken slightly.

4 Put the sauce into a Pyrex dish, add the shrimps and sprinkle with feta and parsley. Bake at 170°C for 10-15 mins.

Mussels with rice *(mydopilafo)*

Ingredients

1 kg mussels (fresh)
2½ cups risotto rice
½ cup white wine
¾ cup olive oil
2 medium sized onions
½ bunch parsley
3-4 tomatoes grated
Salt/freshly ground black pepper

1 With a brush or wire pad clean the mussel shells, take out the small black 'moustache' and rinse well.

2 Place the mussels in a pan with a little water and boil for a few minutes till they open; strain them. Throw away those that do not open.

3 Finely chop the onions and parsley.

4 Sauté the onions in hot oil until they become soft and a light golden colour.

5 Add the mussels and rice, stirring all well 2-3 times with a wooden spoon.

6 Pour in wine and add the tomatoes, parsley and enough water to cook the rice (4-5 cups). Season with salt and pepper.

7 Cook the *mydopilaf* for a while over low heat.

8 Stir a few times until all the water has been absorbed.

9 Remove from the heat, cover, and let it stand for 5 minutes before serving.

Note: This is a very common way to eat mussels in Greece, particularly on the days that traditionally require people to abstain from meat.

Cuttlefish with spinach *(soupies me spanaki)*

Note: a very unusual but delicious dish which is served as a main course in Greece.

Ingredients

1 kg cuttlefish (fresh or frozen)
1-1½ kg spinach (fresh or frozen)
1 onion
4-5 fresh spring onions (and the green stalks)
½ cup dry white wine
½ cup olive oil
1 tomato
1 bunch dill and some fennel
Salt/freshly ground black pepper

1 Clean the cuttlefish: remove bone, eyes, ink bag and insides.

2 Cut the cuttlefish into large pieces and wash well.

3 Wash the spinach well and cut into bid chunks.

4 Chop finely the onion, spring onions, dill and fennel.

5 In a saucepan heat the oil and then…

6 Add onions and cuttlefish and stir a few times.

7 When the water has been absorbed, add wine and tomato (which has been grated or put into the food processor).

8 Allow the cuttlefish to simmer, adding some water if necessary, and when soft…

9 Add spinach and season with salt and pepper.

10 Towards the end of cooking add the chopped dill and fennel.

11 Stir the cuttlefish and spinach once or twice, simmer for another 15 minutes, and then turn off the heat.

12 Allow the dish to cool down a little before serving.

Note: This (like others using cuttlefish) is another traditional Lenten dish in Greece. Perfectly smooth, their taste is very pleasant and unexpectedly sweet, with a tender almost chewy texture.

Sweets and desserts *(glyka)*

In ancient Greece certain foodstuffs were seen as a suitable dessert to be taken with the wine that was drunk after the meal — a single taste of unmixed wine at the moment of libation, followed by plenty of wine mixed with water. Now clean tables — 'second tables'— were brought, on which cakes, sweets, nuts and fresh and dried fruit were served to accompany the wine. These delicacies were called *tragemata*, 'what one chews alongside wine' (a convenient translation is 'dessert').

These days however what is generally referred to as desserts the Greeks call sweets, and they are generally not eaten after a meal as is done in other western countries. They rarely eat a dessert after a meal, and if they do it is most likely to be whichever fresh fruit is in season.

What sets the Greek 'sweets' apart, is their eastern influence. Whereas western desserts are more sponge and cream based, the Greek sweets are sugar based and many include fyllo pastry. Nuts are widely used in many desserts, and then once the dessert is baked, it is drenched in a sweet aromatic honey syrup, as in walnut cake *(karythopita)*. Apart from the beautiful flavours it infuses, the syrup helps to preserve the dessert.

The 'sweets' are generally kept for special occasions — weddings, baptisms, holidays and namedays — and especially when there is a visitor, most often consumed between meals and served with black coffee and a glass of ice-cold water. This way they can savour and enjoy them completely on their own, away from the fullness of a meal, as they are in themselves very filling and a truly sensational taste

Baklava

Notes:
The ingredients are the amounts required for a rectangular oven dish about 40x28 cm.
Traditionally baklava was the special sweet for weddings. On Lesvos they use almonds rather than walnuts; in Turkey they use pistachio, but Daphne prefers walnuts.
Also, while most baklava has syrup over it, Daphne prefers it to be crispy so instead she only uses honey. However, it is important to pour the honey over the baklava while it is piping hot so that it melts and spreads everywhere.

Ingredients:
500 g fyllo pastry
500 g walnuts coarsely chopped
1 cup sugar
1 cup olive oil
1 cup vegetable oil
2 cups honey
1 tbsp ground cinnamon
1 tsp ground cloves

1 Preheat the oven to 170°C

2 In a bowl mix the walnuts, sugar, cinnamon and cloves.

3 Layer the fyllo sheets in the oven dish one by one, sprinkling handfuls of the walnut mixture in between. Start with two sheets at the bottom and finish with three on the top.

4 With a sharp knife cut the baklava into diagonal portions right through to the bottom. Hold it with the other hand while cutting.

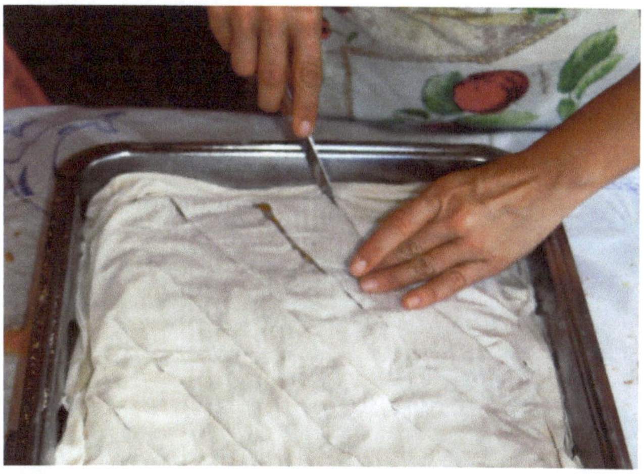

5 Pour both cups of oil over the top and shake the dish a little so that the oil spreads evenly over the whole surface.

6 Bake for 30-35 minutes, until the surface is golden brown.

7 As soon as it is taken out of the oven, pour the honey over the top following the cuts on the surface. Serve at room temperature.

Notes:
– The secret of most traditional sweets is that there are no eggs or milk in the ingredients. Therefore, there is no need to keep them in the fridge. They can be stored in a cool, dry place, covered with cling film.
– In the past women had the time to oil each sheet of *fyllo* with a brush instead of pouring the oil on top as Daphne suggests.
– Traditionally the baklava is very sweet but Daphne says her husband, Iannis, has been very influenced by the European concept of "cutting down on sugar". So, if there is a Iannis at home then ¾ cup sugar and 1½ cup honey will 'Europeanize' the baklava!

Orange fyllo pie *(portokalopita)*

Notes:
– This pie (or cake) is a soft, golden-coloured dessert that one encounters all around Greece.
– Because one needs orange zest it is best to use organically grown fruit (see Votsala marmalade on page 133).
– The vanilla used can be either two split pods or natural extract.

Ingredients

250 gr Greek yogurt
1 cup vegetable oil
1 cup sugar
4 eggs
1 tsp vanilla extract
2 tbsp baking powder
500 gr fyllo pastry
Zest of 3 oranges

For the syrup:
2 cups of sugar
2 cups of water
1 cinnamon stick
2 cups of orange juice
2 tbsp orange zest

1 Tear up the *fyllo* sheets into small pieces and let them dry so that they do not stick together when used later.

2 Grate the outer skin of the unwaxed oranges to obtain the zest. Put 2 tablespoonfuls aside for the syrup.

3 Start by preparing the syrup. In a pot combine the water and sugar with the cinnamon stick. Bring to the boil for about 5 minutes. Take off the heat and add the orange juice and the zest. Set aside to cool completely.

4 In a large bowl combine everything except the *fyllo* and the zest. Whisk for 2-3 minutes. Incorporate the torn *fyllo* into the batter a little at a time, using a rubber spatula. If you add all the pieces at once they will clump together.

5 Mix in the zest and then pour it all into a greased baking pan. Bake in a preheated oven at 180°C for about 50 minutes until the top is brown.

6 Remove from the oven and pierce the top in a number of places with a long clean skewer.

7 Pour the cooled syrup onto the hot pie, one ladle at a time. Allow this to be absorbed into the pie before adding the next ladle. Repeat until all of the syrup has been used. It is essential to distribute the syrup evenly around the pie.

8 Allow the pie to cool to room temperature before serving. It is particularly good accompanied by some vanilla ice cream or Greek yogurt.

Nut pastry (kadaifi)

Notes:

– *Kadaifi* pastry is in fact finely shredded *fyllo* pastry which looks a little like very fine vermicelli noodles or shredded wheat. This threadlike dough is widely used in Greek baking for confectionery and alongside baklava, is one of the most popular Greek desserts.

– Two typical Greek sweet options involve filling or layering *kadaifi* with a mild young cheese (see Daphne's recipe for *kioufene* on page 135) or with a paste of chopped nuts, sugar and cinnamon (see following recipe which is not one of Daphne's but is included here for obvious reasons). This is baked and then drenched in a sugar syrup flavoured with lemon juice.

– *Kadaifi* is not easy to find in the West even online. However, most Greek, Arab and Turkish grocery shops stock frozen packs of the pastry.

– The pastry needs to be defrosted thoroughly in the fridge or according to the instructions on the packaging. One needs to work relatively quickly with it and, crucially, take a liberal approach to the amount of melted butter used.

Ingredients

Filling:
300 g coarsely chopped walnuts or almonds
50 g sugar
1 egg slightly beaten
2 tbsp brandy
1 tsp cinnamon (for walnut filling) or
1 tbsp lemon zest (for almond filling)

Pastry:
400 g kadaifi
150 g unsalted butter, melted
1 tbsp cinnamon for top (optional)

Syrup:
400 g caster sugar
400 ml water
1 tbsp lemon juice
1-2 pieces lemon rind

1 In a bowl mix the chopped nuts and other filling ingredients.

2 Grease a deep rectangular baking dish with butter.

3 Spread out the *kadaifi* pastry, carefully disentangle and divide into thick strips about 20 cm long.

4 Put a large tablespoon of the filling at one end of a strip and roll up carefully, starting at this end. With one's fingers guide the strings of pastry at the edges so that they stay secure. The result should be a cylindrical fat roll about 10 cm long.

5 Place these rolls with their seam downward in the baking dish, leaving a little space between them.

6 Melt the butter and pour about one tablespoon over each roll.

7 Bake in a preheated oven at 180°C for about 40 minutes until they are golden brown. Let them cool while making the syrup.

8 Dissolve the sugar in the water, add the lemon juice and the rind, and boil gently for about 10 minutes, until the syrup thickens slightly. The lemon juice prevents crystals from forming.

9 Allow the *kadaifi* to cool thoroughly before slowly pouring the hot syrup over them. Set aside for some hours until the syrup is completely absorbed.

Votsala orange marmalade

Notes:
– This recipe is a special of Daphne's mother-in-law. Compared to recipes in cookery books and on the internet, Daphne says that the secret is the cooking of the whole fruit which keeps the aroma and also results in a less bitter rind.
– Oranges are generally coated with paraffin wax that slows down moisture loss and spoilage. So, use organic oranges, otherwise change the boiling water an additional 2-3 times.

Ingredients
Oranges
1 lemon for every 5 oranges
2 mandarins (equivalent to 1 orange)
4 cups sugar for each 5 of fruit pulp

1 Wash the fruit and put it whole into a deep saucepan with cold water. Bring to the boil.

2 At the same time, on another hotplate, boil a second pan of hot water. After the fruit has boiled for a short time transfer it to this second pan and discard the water. This is repeated 4-5 times, always adding fresh water to the empty pan.

3 When the fruit is soft (test with toothpick) take it off the heat. With a perforated spoon transfer each piece of fruit to a bowl of cold water.

4 Change the water at least 4-5 times: this will reduce the bitterness of the fruit.

5 Cut the fruit into halves and scoop out the flesh and put it into a food strainer or spaghetti colander.

6 Press the fruit so that the pulp is collected in a large bowl and the pips and skin remain in the strainer.

7 Keep more than half the peel and cut it into matchstick-like strips.

8 Measure the pulp and put it into a large pan. For every piece of fruit boiled and pulped add the juice of one orange. Also add the chopped peel.

9 For every 5 cups of fruit pulp add 1 cup of sugar.

10 Put the pan on heat and stir continuously until thick.

11 When the marmalade is ready take it off the heat. Ladle it into hot sterilised jars and make sure to fill to the top. Close immediately with air-tight seals.

Sweet cheese pie *(kiounefe)*

Notes:

– The origin of this dish is southern Turkey, where a local cheese is used. What is important is that the cheese should be unsalted and ideally melt and stretch when heated. So, mozzarella works well.

– What makes this different from other syrupy desserts is that it must be eaten hot, right after it is cooked.

Ingredients

400 g kadaifi pastry (see page 132)
100 g butter, melted
250 g mozzarella
1 tbsp flour
Handful of pine nuts
Syrup:
400 g caster sugar
400 ml water
1 tbsp lemon juice
1-2 pieces of lemon rind

1 Start by preparing the syrup. Dissolve the sugar in the water, add the lemon juice and rind, and bring to the boil.

2 Reduce the heat and allow it to simmer for about 10-15 minutes until it gets a little thicker. Take it off the heat and set aside to cool completely.

3 Take a non-stick frying pan (about 30 cm diameter) and cover the bottom with 2-3 tablespoons of softened butter, one tablespoon of flour, and a teaspoon of cold water. Mix the ingredients with the palm of one's hand so that it becomes a roux or thick batter that covers the entire surface.

4 Sprinkle pine nuts over this.

5 Pull the *kataifi* apart so that it becomes 'fluffier' and form a layer about 5 mm thick in the pan.

6 Over the top of this layer of *kataifi* sprinkle shredded mozzarelle or other unsalted cheese. Cover this with another layer of pastry and press it down by hand.

7 Put the pan onto a moderate to low heat until the edges turn a golden brown. Using a large plate turn the pastry upside down.

8 Add 2-3 tablespoons of butter to the pan and slide the *kiounefe* in so that the other side gets browned. As soon as it is ready take it off the heat and pour the cool syrup over it. Serve immediately, ideally with some ice cream or whipped cream.

9 As an alternative to using pine nuts, a garnish or topping of ground or crushed pistachios is often used.

Walnut cake *(karidopita)*

Note: This dessert, popular throughout Greece, has several variations — almost every recipe one looks up has slightly different ingredients. Some use cloves rather than nutmeg, some use less eggs (one 'theory' is that one egg, one tablespoon of sugar, and one tablespoon of semolina is used for each tablespoon of walnuts), some add orange zest, some use more brandy in the cake and add a little to the syrup.

Ingredients

8 eggs, separated
2½ cups coarsely ground walnuts
½ cup fine semolina
4 tsp self-raising flour
250 g butter
1 cup sugar
½ tsp cinnamon
½ tsp ground nutmeg
3 tsp baking powder
A dash of brandy

For the syrup:
2½ cups sugar
3 cups water
Juice of ½ a lemon

1 Cream the butter and sugar until light and fluffy.

2 Add the egg yolks one by one, beating each addition so that it is well incorporated. Sift in the flour, semolina, baking powder and spices.

4 Add walnuts and brandy and mix all well.

5 Beat egg white until stiff and fold gently into batter.

6 Butter and flour a baking dish. Fill with the batter and bake in a pre-heated oven at 180°C for about 50 minutes.

7 Make the syrup while the cake is baking. Place all the ingredients in a heavy-based saucepan and stir while being heated until the sugar dissolves.

8 Bring to boil over moderate heat for about 10 minutes or until syrup starts to thicken.

9 Pour the hot syrup evenly all over the hot cake so that it is fully absorbed.

10 Let the cake stand for about 20 minutes and then serve, ideally with some ice cream or whipped cream on the side.

Custard pie with syrup
(galaktoboureko)

Notes:
– *Galaktoboureko* is at its best eaten fresh, preferably while still warm, but it is still good the next day.
– Although almonds are not in most traditional versions of this pie, they are included in Daphne's recipe below and if used do give extra flavour and crunchiness.

Ingredients

1 kg fyllo pastry
½ kg blanched almonds
125 g butter (to brush on fyllo)

For the custard:
1½ l milk
1¼ cups fine semolina
1 cup sugar
7 eggs
2 tbsp butter
3 lemons
For the syrup:
2 cups sugar
1 cup water
1-2 tsp vanilla essence

1 Heat the milk.

2 In a saucepan mix the semolina and sugar. Pour in the heated milk and stir until the mixture thickens.

4 Grate the outer skin of the unwaxed lemons to obtain the zest.

5 Beat the eggs lightly in a bowl.

6 Add the eggs, lemon zest and 2 tablespoons of butter into the custard. Mix all the ingredients very well.

7 Butter an oven dish and lay two sheets of *fyllo* pastry over this, brushing them with melted butter. Continue laying half of the packet of *fyllo* brushing each sheet with butter and sprinkling with almonds.

8 Pour in the custard mixture.

9 Layer the remaining sheets of *fyllo* buttering each one and sprinkling with almonds.

10 The top two sheets should be buttered as before but not sprinkled with almonds.

11 With a small sharp knife score a pattern of diamonds or squares in the size of the intended portions into the top layer, and then sprinkle tiny drops of water on top of the pastry to stop it curling up at the edges.

12 Bake at 200°C for approximately an hour and 15 minutes, or until the pastry puffs up and turns golden brown and crisp.

13 Meanwhile prepare the syrup: dissolve the sugar in the water and when it thickens (it takes about 9 minutes) add the vanilla essence.

14 When the pie has been taken out of the oven, slowly pour the syrup all over it.

15 Let stand for a while to allow the syrup to be absorbed, then cut and serve.

Rice pudding *(rizogalo)*

Notes:
– Traditional Greek rice pudding is a homely, comforting no butter, egg free thick and creamy treat — it takes quite a bit of stirring action to thicken properly, but the end result is really worth the effort. It gets its name from its two main ingredients — rice (*rizi*) and milk (*gala*) — and it is usually flavoured with vanilla and lemon or orange rinds.
– The traditional recipe for Greek rice pudding calls for a kind of rice called '*glase*', which is usually used in soups; the next best is to use Arborio rice.

Ingredients
5 cups milk
2 cups water
½ cup risotto rice
¾ cup sugar
2 tbsp corn flour
1 tsp vanilla essence
Rind of a lemon or orange
1 pinch mastic powder (optional)
cinnamon for garnishing

1 Heat the water, rice, lemon or orange rinds and, if using it, the mastic powder in a large heavy bottomed saucepan.

2 When the rice has absorbed the water add 4 cups of milk and cook on a low heat, stirring constantly until the rice is soft.

3 Take out the rinds.

4 In the remaining cup of milk dissolve the sugar and corn flour. Pour this into the saucepan and mix well. Continue cooking on low heat, stirring occasionally until the pudding thickens.

5 Take off the heat and spoon the *rizogalo* into individual bowls, allow it to cool then cover with cling film and store in the fridge.

6 Serve as a delicious dessert or mid-day snack with a sprinkle of cinnamon.

Note: Some years ago at the end of the summer season, during a Votsala 'family' trip to Portugal, Iannis and Daphne tried to convince Rudina (the wife of Spyros who does the grilling at the barbecues, helps with breakfasts, and is the general handyman) that she would do a good job of the cooking. Spyros agrees and tries to encourage her but Rudina is hesitant and wonders how she will manage. Years have passed and Roudy (as she is known by everyone) has become an excellent cook who produces wonderful 'surprise' dishes for breakfast every day. The tartlets on the following page are an example.

Rudina's custard tartlets

Notes:
– There will always be some *fyllo* left and it can be kept in the fridge wrapped in cling film for a few days. For a longer period, it should be frozen.
– Vanilla sugar is, as its name suggests, sugar that has been scented with vanilla. It is often used in baking to add vanilla flavouring to cakes and cookies or can be used to sprinkle over fresh or cooked fruits or even added to coffee. In many European countries vanilla sugar is sold in small sachets or envelopes. Less common in the UK but it is available in 8 or 10g packs from Tesco, eBay and Amazon. It is very fine sugar and generally used for baking as vanilla extract is less common. You can replace one sachet of vanilla sugar with 1-2 teaspoons of vanilla extract.

***Ingredients** (for 12 tartlets)*

500 ml fresh cream
500 ml fresh milk
160 g sugar
1 egg + 6 egg yolks
1 tbsp cornflour
butter: a little to grease tart pan
150 g (approx.) fyllo pastry
Icing sugar & cinnamon for garnishing

1 In a medium saucepan heat both the cream and milk.

2 In a bowl mix sugar and eggs well.

3 Pour this mixture into the pan and stir.

4 Dissolve the cornflour in a little cold water, add the vanilla and pour into pan.

5 Mix the creamy sauce well with a whisk until it thickens, then take it off the heat.

6 Butter the tart pan/tray or cases (if separate cases are used) well.

7 Take 4 sheets of *fyllo* and cut them into three in both directions, ie 9 small squares x 4 = a total of 36 pieces. This allows 3 pieces for each tartlet.

8 In each cup of the tartlet tray (or each pastry case) place three pieces of *fyllo* one above the other in (as Daphne says) "an artistic way."

9 Fill each tartlet with cream.

10 Bake in a preheated oven at 180°C for about 30 - 40 minutes until the tartlets turn golden brown.

11 Take out of tray, cool on a rack and serve with a sprinkling of icing sugar and cinnamon.

Milk pie *(galatopita)*

Note: *Galatopita* recipes tend to hail from the Peloponnese and northern parts of the country. It is one of those humble, yet succulent desserts most Greeks love. As one cook has written, "its simplicity is what makes it so good."

Ingredients

500 g fyllo pastry
8 eggs
6 cups of milk
200 g Greek yoghurt
1 cup sugar
Butter to brush on the filo
Icing sugar
Cinnamon

1 Beat the eggs and then mix them with the yoghurt, milk, and half a cup of sugar. Beat all well.

2 Brush an oven dish with melted butter. Then as evenly as possible spread half the *fyllo*, one sheet at a time, brushing each one with melted butter, over the base of the dish. Sprinkle each layer with sugar and cinnamon.

3 Pour the milk mixture into the dish and then layer the other half of the *fyllo* pastry. Brush each sheet with butter on the worktop and then place it carefully on the top of the pie. It is not possible to brush the *fyllo* after it has been laid in place because the filling is so liquid.

4 Remember to sprinkle sugar and cinnamon on each sheet, but not the top, which only needs to be brushed with butter.

5 Bake in a preheated oven at medium temperature, 160°C, until the top is golden brown.

6 Serve the pie hot and possibly sprinkled with icing sugar and cinnamon.

Note: The favourite Greek street food and snack, *bougatsa*, (see following recipe) is traditionally made with very large handmade *fyllo* sheets. The sheets are rolled super thin and then are folded over multiple times before finally being folded over the filling. They are sometimes made as individual parcels, perfect for eating on the go.
Although *bougatsa* and *galaktoboureko* (see page 138) are both custard desserts encased in fyllo, one of the major differences is that the latter is soaked in syrup. *Bougatsa* on the other hand is usually dusted with cinnamon and icing sugar and has no syrup.

Custard pastry *(bougatsa)*

Notes: *Bougatsa* is a very crispy pastry filled with a velvety custard cream. Always served warm, sprinkled with lots of icing sugar and cinnamon. The filling is rich, so it is usually eaten as a snack on its own or with a cup of coffee rather than as a dessert. Greek often have it for breakfast! Not one of Daphne's recipes, but included here for fairly obvious reasons.

***Ingredients** (for 4 portions)*
5 fyllo sheets
70 g butter (melted)
Cinnamon
Icing sugar

For the custard filling
½ l whole fresh milk
70 g fine semolina
80 g sugar
Salt (very little)
1 tbsp vanilla extract
15 g butter
Lemon zest
2 eggs (yolks only)

1 Put the milk into a pan over medium heat, and add the sugar in the middle without stirring.

2 When the milk starts to boil add the semolina and now stir constantly with a whisk allowing it to simmer for about 6-8 minutes until thickened.

3 Remove from the heat and add the vanilla extract, a little lemon zest, and cold butter. Stir until the butter has melted.

4 Add the two egg yolks, with a little salt, and stir.

5 Cover the custard with cling film and allow to become completely cool. Make sure that the cling film touches the surface of the custard so that it does not form a crust while it cools.

6 Lightly brush a baking pan (20 x 25 cm) with melted butter.

7 Line the bottom of the pan with 5 sheets of *fyllo,* brushing each well with melted butter. Lay them alternatively lengthways and allow about half of each sheet to overlap the pan.

8 Add the custard filling, spreading it evenly. Fold the overlapping *fyllo* sheets over the top, brushing each with melted butter.

9 Bake in a preheated oven at 180°C for about 40-50 minutes, until the pastry is golden brown and crispy on top and the filling has set.

10 Leave it to cool slightly and then sprinkle with icing sugar and cinnamon. It is best eaten while still warm.

Kourabiedes

Notes:
–These, and the following *melomakarona*, are cakes or biscuits traditionally made at Christmas. In every Greek home large decorative platefuls of them are found.
– The *kourabiedes* ('snowy shortbread') are found all year round in cake shops (*zaharoplastio)* and are used for various occasions such as namedays, baptisms and weddings. There are many versions, those in the Sporades for example are made with egg yolks, brandy, rose water, baking powder and caster sugar. Daphne prefers the simple version given below that originates from Lesvos, and their taste brings back fond memories for her.

Ingredients

½ kg butter
1 cup icing sugar
½ cup blanched almonds
Flour — about 1kg plus a little more

1 Roughly chop the almonds and toast them in the oven until golden brown.

2 Cream butter that has been cooled in the fridge — beat it until it is light and fluffy.

3 Slowly add the icing sugar to the butter, beating continuously.

4 Add the roasted almonds & mix well.

5 Gradually add flour and fold it all together until combined to form a dough. It may be necessary to knead in the last of the flour by hand but don't over mix the dough, which should not stick to one's hands, while being soft and workable.

6 Take small amounts of dough, about the size of a table-tennis ball, pat them into a round shape and then flatten slightly. Place them on grease-proof paper on an oven dish. Repeat until all the pastry is finished.

7 Bake in a preheated oven at 180ºC for about 40 minutes. They are ready when the underside becomes golden brown (check by turning one over).

8 Sift some icing sugar onto a large plate and place the *kourabiedes* on it while still hot and sift more icing sugar all over them.

Honey-dipped biscuits
(melomakarona)

Note: Daphne warns that one must be careful with the flour because the recipes of her grandmother and her mother-in-law say "as much as it takes." So, more or less flour may be needed to get a soft and elastic dough that does not stick to the hands.

Ingredients

3 cups olive oil
1 cup sugar
½ cup brandy
½ cup orange juice
1 tsp baking powder
1 tsp bicarbonate of soda
1 tbsp honey
2 handfuls roughly ground walnuts
Ground cinnamon
½ tbsp orange zest
Flour, about 750 g

For the syrup:
¾ cup honey
¾ cup water
1 cup sugar
1 stick cinnamon

1 Put the oil and sugar into a deep bowl.

2 Dissolve the soda in the orange juice and the baking powder in the brandy, and then add both to the bowl.

3 Chop the walnuts and put some aside. Add the rest, the honey and the orange zest to the mixture.

4 Mix all the ingredient well and gradually add the flour, kneading the dough by hand until it becomes soft and elastic. Be careful not to overwork the dough because this can make the *melomakorona* too hard.

5 Take portions of the dough the size of small eggs and pat them into an oval shape. Arrange them on a baking tray leaving room for them to spread.

6 Bake in a preheated oven at 180°C for about 20 minutes until they are golden brown.

7 Meanwhile prepare the syrup: put the water, honey, sugar and cinnamon stick into a saucepan and stir well. Put on a low heat and bring to the boil 2 or 3 times then remove from the heat.

8 One at a time dip the *melomakarona* into the syrup using a slotted spoon. Take them out immediately and arrange them on a plate. Sprinkle with cinnamon (optional) and the remaining walnuts.

Almond biscuits *(amygdalota)*

Notes:

– The almond tree flourishes in a dry climate with very little water, which makes it ideal for Greece, especially in the south and on many of the islands.

– *Amygdalota* in particular is a treat that symbolizes new beginnings. As its name suggests (*amygdalo* = almond), this traditional sweet, which is slightly crisp outside and soft and moist on the inside, is prepared with finely chopped or ground almonds (in some cases bitter almonds are also used) and sugar, and flavoured with scented flower water (usually rose or orange blossom) or an essential oil like tangerine, vanilla or mastic. Egg whites and semolina are sometimes added in the recipe to create a denser texture. As a final touch, many are covered with a dusting of icing sugar. One could say it is the Greek version of marzipan, although *amygdalota* differs both in flavour and texture.

– Like many desserts in Greece, there are seemingly endless variations, some are baked and some not: the recipe, which determines their shape — pear shapes are very popular — texture and flavour, depends on the region from which they originate.

Ingredients

400 g ground blanched almonds
100 g sugar
2 egg whites
50 ml rose water
Icing sugar for dusting
Some cloves or flaked almonds for decoration (optional)

1 In a bowl mix the ground almonds and sugar together well.

2 Beat the egg whites till they form soft peaks. Fold the beaten egg whites gently into the almond and sugar mixture.

3 Form small almond shaped balls, or preferred shapes, by hand and place them on a prepared baking tray.

4 Bake in a preheated oven at about 120°C for 20-25 minutes, until they are firm on the outside and golden in colour.

5 As soon as they come out of the oven spray them with rose water. When they have cooled down roll them in icing sugar.

Note: this is not a Daphne recipe but it seemed sensible to put it with the other biscuits.

Appendix 1

Over the years my wife Sonia and I have visited Greece, and in particular Mykonos and Crete — other than Lesbos — on many occasions and at one time spent Christmas and New Year there for nine consecutive years. Because of my work this was the best time for us to escape on holiday. The main problem is that at this time of the year there are very few tavernas open and, in some places, certainly not our favourite ones. However, we were usually fortunate to find tavernas that served good and 'real' Greek food.

Most of the good traditional cooking we grew to love — pork with celery, stuffed cabbage leaves in egg-lemon sauce and *soutsoukakia* for example — we learnt to cook with Daphne, but there are some that we didn't and I have taken the liberty of including recipes for them here.

Garlic sauce *(skordalia)*

Note:
Although this is not a recipe from Daphne, this simple garlic dish is found everywhere in Greece and is an accompaniment par excellence for beetroot, salt cod (see page 153) and fried slices of zucchini and aubergine (see page 150). There are several variations, some with ground almonds, some with a potato base, and others use bread — some say it must be white, some believe it should be really good sourdough and there are even some who prefer to use whole-wheat or multigrain and do not mind the darker colour. There are also recipes that add walnuts.

Ingredients
4-5 slices of stale bread
4 cloves of garlic
200 ml of extra virgin olive oil
Juice of 1 lemon or red wine vinegar
55 g finely crushed walnuts (optional)

1 Soak the bread (crusts removed) in water for about 10 minutes and squeeze out the excess.

2 Peel and slice the garlic. The number of cloves used depends on their size and on how potent one wants the sauce to be.

3 Traditionally the garlic is crushed by pestle in a mortar, but it is obviously easier to blend the moist bread, garlic, lemon juice and salt in a food processor at its lowest setting, gradually adding the olive oil.

4 The *skordalia* tastes best if left for a day to allow the flavours to blend. Serve separately in a bowl, for people to use as much as they want. If too thick it can be thinned with a little water.

Note:
To make *skordalia* with potato instead of bread, follow the same recipe but in place of the bread use about 500 g of potatoes cut into cubes and boiled in water until soft. It is essential that the potatoes are hot, because if they are cold it can be difficult to combine the ingredients and the sauce may be lumpy.

Fried aubergine and zucchini *(melitzanes ke kolokythakia tiganita)*

Note: This is another simple dish that is probably the most popular *meze* for Greeks and is found almost all year round in virtually every taverna. In some places it is served with *skordalia* and in others with *tzatziki*. The form of coating used varies from a minimalistic one of old-fashioned plain flour and seasoning to a tempura type batter. Some slice the zucchini and aubergines across into round discs while others prefer to slice them lengthwise.

Ingredients
3-4 aubergine/zucchini (about 450 g)
Salt/freshly ground black pepper
Olive oil or vegetable oil for deep frying

Batter for frying:
1 cup flour
1 tbsp cornflour/corn starch (optional)
Freshly ground black pepper
See also note at right.

1 The aubergine or zucchini should be sliced thinly into round discs (or lengthwise if preferred), salted on both sides, and left in a colander to drain for at least 30 minutes.

2 Preheat the oil in a pan or deep-fryer. It is essential to heat the oil enough — the perfect temperature is around 180°C.

3 Prepare the batter. The simplest version is to mix some pepper with flour and the slices that are to be deep fried in a large plastic bag. Shake the bag for a minute or so until flour completely covers all the slices.

4 For crispy slices it is best to fry them in batches, not overcrowding the pan, until golden on both sides. Remove with a slotted spoon and place on paper towel to absorb excess oil.

5 Serve immediately together with a bowl of *skordalia* or *tzatziki*.

Note: A light batter is made of iced water (sometimes sparkling water is used to keep the batter light) and soft flour. Eggs (especially egg yolk), baking soda or baking powder, cornflour and/or spices may also be added. Tempura batter is traditionally mixed in small batches using chopsticks for only a few seconds, leaving lumps in the mixture that, along with the cold batter temperature, result in the unique fluffy and crisp tempura structure when cooked. The batter is often kept cold by adding ice, or by placing the bowl inside a larger bowl with ice in it. Make sure that the aubergine or zucchini slices are thoroughly dry to ensure that the batter stays crisp.

Dolmades in egg-lemon sauce *(dolmades avgolemono)*

Note: When the stuffed vine leaves are served with *avgolemono* it usually means they contain minced meat. In Greece the vegetarian version is very rarely served with this sauce.
See also the recipe for vegetarian dolmades on page 66.

Ingredients

225 g fresh vine leaves
500 g minced lamb or beef
1 cups of risotto rice
1 large onion
2-3 spring onions
3-4 tbsp mint
3-4 tbsp parsley
3-4 tbsp dill
1 lemon
½ cup of good quality olive oil
Salt/freshly ground black pepper

Avgolemono sauce: the ingredients and preparation all as described on pages 83 and 84.

1 Put the vine leaves into boiling water for about a minute. When they have changed colour take them out with a perforated spoon and leave them to cool. Be careful not to let them boil as them may disintegrate and be difficult to handle.

2 Finely chop the onion, spring onions, parsley, mint and dill.

3 Squeeze the lemon removing any pips.

4 In a large bowl, mix together the minced meat, rice, onion, parsley, dill, mint, lemon juice and half the oil.

5 Spread the vine leaves out smooth side down and remove any remaining stalks before preparing the *dolmades* as described on page 66. After this lay each *dolma* on the spread leaves at the bottom of a saucepan cover them with water, adding the remaining oil, and cook them all as described on the same page.

6 While the *dolmades* are cooking it is time to prepare the egg-lemon sauce and this should be done as described on page 84.

7 In Greece the sauce is usually poured over the *dolmades* once they have cooled a little. The saucepan should be shaken so that the sauce gets well amalgamated. However, there are those who prefer to serve the sauce separately.

Kleftiko 2

Notes:
– See also alternative version on page 114 and 115.
– This recipe is one that the author has used successfully for a number of years, inspired by the version enjoyed on a number of occasions at Nikos Taverna on Mykonos. The quantities given are for making six servings.

Ingredients

6 lamb fillets or shanks
3 carrots
3 large or 6 medium potatoes
1 large onion
2 large tomatoes
6-12 cubes of feta cheese
6-12 garlic cloves
Juice of 1 lemon
150 ml olive oil
½ tsp dried oregano
½ tsp dried thyme
6 sprigs of rosemary
Salt/freshly ground black pepper
Greaseproof paper, aluminium foil, and string

1 Make incisions in the meat and insert slivers (or cloves) of garlic.

2 In a bowl mix the olive oil, lemon juice, herbs and pepper. Add the lamb to the mixture, turning it so that it is coated on all sides. Cover and marinade for a few hours or overnight in the fridge.

3 Cut the potatoes and carrots in half. Cut the peeled onion and the tomatoes into thick slices.

4 Spread out the sheets (about 30+ cm square) of greaseproof paper and arrange slices of potato and carrot with one or two cubes of feta in the centre of each. On top of this place a piece of lamb with some of its marinade. On the meat add a large slice of tomato drizzle with some olive oil, a slice of onion, and a sprig of rosemary.

5 Gather the edges together to form a pouch, pour in a little of any remaining marinade, twist the top of the pouch tightly and then, ideally, wrap this in a similar pouch of aluminium foil, tied at the top with string.

6 Place the pouches in a shallow oven pan and bake in a preheated oven at 150-160ºC for 2-3 hours.

Note: It is possible to add some other vegetables, for example a piece of celery and/or a slice of pepper. One can also add a little wine to the marinade but be careful not to add to much liquid because it could spill out of the pouches.

Salt cod with garlic sauce
(bakaliaros skordalia)

Notes:
– The idea of dried and salted cod may be a bit daunting for some but this preserved fish has been a popular ingredient in many different cuisines for hundreds of years. The scarcity of fridges and the cheapness of the cod were the original reasons.
– On the 25th of March, Greeks celebrate Independence Day and The Annunciation of the Virgin Mary. This is one of the few days on which fish is allowed to be eaten during the time of the Great Lent; a period when it is custom to abstain from meat, fish, eggs and dairy produce. Traditionally, on this day Greeks eat a deep-fried, lightly battered salted cod dipped into a garlic sauce (*skordalia*). This popular dish is also widely eaten during the winter. The recipe for the garlic sauce can be found on page 149.
– The fish can be bought either filleted or un-filleted and it is said that the latter has a nicer flavour.

Ingredients *(for 3 or 4 servings)*

1 piece of salt cod, approx. 750 gr

Batter
250 ml beer or soda water
120 gr plain flour
1 egg white
Vegetable oil for deep frying

1 If the cod is not already cut up, cut it into medium size pieces, discard fins and tail if these are included.

2 Soak the cod for at least 24 hours in a bowl of cold water, starting the evening before it is to be eaten. Change the water 3-4 times to extract the salt.

3 Rinse and drain the pieces. Then skin (it said that ideally this is better) and if necessary bone the if not already filleted.

4 Add some black pepper to the flour and then mix in the beer or soda water to get a smooth batter. Set aside for about an hour.

5 Beat the egg white until stiff and fold it into the batter.

6 Empty all the cod pieces into the batter, and one at a time deep-fry in very hot oil until golden. Drain on paper towel. Serve with lemon wedges and a bowl of *skordalia.*

Note: There are many opinions regarding the batter, see also the notes for fried aubergine and zucchini on page 150.

Stuffed scallops *(ktenia gemista)*

Ingredients

1 kg scallops in their shells
1 onion
2 spring onions
1 ripe tomato
Zest of 1 small orange
1 bunch parsley
½ cup of long-grained rice
3 tbsp bulgur (optional)
75 ml ouzo
1 tsp ground cumin
250 ml olive oil
500 ml water
Salt/freshly ground black pepper

1 Scrub the scallops under cold running water to remove any sand. Put them into a saucepan with a little water and let them boil for 5 minutes. When they start opening, take them out and set them aside.

2 Strain the liquid released through a cheesecloth-lined strainer and reserve.

3 Shuck the scallops — the skill used to remove the meat from the shell — taking care not to separate the shells. Run a knife along the inside of the shell to separate it from the meat. Then run the knife around the white scallop meat and pink roe, removing the skirt and black stomach sac. Bin all this excess material so only the white juicy meat and pink roe are left.

4 Blanch the shells in boiling water and set aside.

5 Cut the white flesh into 2-3 pieces and return to the shell with the roe.

6 Chop the onion and parsley finely, cut the spring onions into thin roundels and peel, deseed and chop the tomato.

7 Heat half the oil in a frying pan and sauté the onion and spring onions, as well as the rice (and bulgur, if using it). Pour the ouzo over this and add the tomato, cumin, orange zest and parsley. Season to taste.

8 Let the stuffing simmer for a few minutes, then take it off the heat and fill each scallop shell with the mixture, incorporating the scallop flesh. Cover each shell with its lid.

9 Arrange the shells in a wide saucepan in layers, pour over the reserved cooking water and the rest of the olive oil. Cover with a plate to keep then from opening while cooking.

10 Cover the saucepan and let the scallops simmer until all the water has been absorbed and only the oil remains at the bottom of the pan.

Spoon sweets *(glyka tou koutaliou)*

Notes:

– Spoon sweets are a form of preserve. Fruit preserves first appeared in the Greek cuisine in the Byzantine era and particularly gained a place in Ottoman times, when sugar became readily available. They can be made from almost any fruit, though sour and bitter fruits are especially prized. There are also spoon sweets produced without fruit.

– Many fruits or parts of fruits that are normally inedible, such as the various citrus peels and blossoms, or sliced citrus fruits with their peel intact, can be made into sweet, flavourful preserves, as can some vegetables such as baby eggplants or cherry tomatoes.

– A traditional and delightful Greek custom is the offering of spoon sweets to guests as a symbol of hospitality usually served with Greek coffee and a glass of cold water. They are called spoon sweets because the usual serving size is a well-filled teaspoon.

– Whole fruit preserves can be found in most Greek homes. They are made by slowly and gently boiling fruit in water and sugar over several hours or days, until the syrup sets. So, the main prerequisites to making good spoon sweets are said to be "patience and a heavy pot". Some lemon juice is often added to preserve the fruit's original colour, as the citric acid prevents oxidation. A small quantity of blanched almonds, slivered or whole, may also be added for crunch, often to baby eggplants, apples or grapes.

– It is impossible to provide a single recipe for all spoon sweets. The liquid and sugar measurements vary according to the type of fruit or vegetable used. They are not as dense as jam or jelly. The fruit should remain firm and sit in a nice pool of syrup thick enough to coat a spoon. A well-made spoon sweet retains the original shape, colour, aroma and taste of the fruit.

– Spoon sweets are prepared all over Greece, and some varieties are tied to specific regions. The island of Aegina, for example, is famous for their pistachio spoon sweet.

– A wide range of spoon sweets is now commercially produced but women committed to the preservation of traditional recipes and preparation methods feared a loss of their culture and identity, so they formed local Women's Agricultural Cooperatives all over Greece. Traditional homemade spoon sweets are now widely available through these Cooperatives.

Sour cherry preserve *(vyssino glyko)*

Notes:
– This is the most common of the Greek spoon sweets and also the most traditional.
– Sour cherries are great for cooking. They are richly flavoured and firm of flesh so that they don't go mushy during cooking. There are two main varieties (groups of cultivars) of the sour cherry: the dark-red morello cherry and the lighter-red amarelle cherry.
– Both are delicious with vanilla ice cream, mixed with thick Greek yogurt or as a topping on cheesecake. These cherries are also delightful served with cheese.

Ingredients:
1 kg sour cherries
1 kg sugar
2 cups water
1 tbs lemon juice

1 Wash the cherries and extract the stones, carefully keeping the cherries intact. This is the hardest part of the recipe but there is a special tool (cherry and olive pitter) that can be used.

2 Place the stones in the water as they are taken out, and when all the cherries have been done remove the stones but do not discard the water.

3 In a large, wide saucepan spread about one fifth of the cherries. Sprinkle about a fifth of the sugar over them. Repeat, layering cherries and sugar until both are used up.

4 Add the water to the saucepan and boil for about twenty minutes. Skim off the scum with a slotted spoon.

5 Take off the heat and let them stand in their syrup overnight.

6 Next day add the lemon juice, bring back to the boil until it reaches its setting point ie until the syrup is thick enough to coat the back of a spoon.

7 Remove from heat and allow to cool. Put the mixture into sterilized jars and seal tightly.

Plain fritters with honey sauce *(loukoumades)*

Notes:
– These are perfectly round, bite-sized, balls of dough deep fried, crispy and golden on the outside, but fluffy and airy inside. Coated with honey and sprinkled with cinnamon.
– The *loukoumades* should ideally be eaten hot before the honey gets a chance to soak in and make them soggy.

Ingredients
225 g plain flour
Yeast (14 g fresh or 6 g dried)
300 ml warm water
½ tsp sugar
¼ tsp salt
Vegetable oil for frying
6 tbsp (approx.) thyme honey (ideally)
Ground cinnamon

1 Dissolve the yeast (if fresh is being used) in half a cup of warm (not hot) water, add the sugar to activate it and let it stand for about 10 minutes.

2 Sift the flour and salt into a bowl, then add the activated yeast (or dried yeast) into it mixing continuously. Slowly pour in the warm water while continuing to beat the dough until it starts to bubble.

3 Cover the bowl and allow it to rest in a warm place for about 2½ hours to allow the dough to double in volume.

4 Heat plenty of oil in a deep pan.

5 Wet a teaspoon in cold water so that dough will not stick on it and scoop up a ball of the dough. With one's hand push it down gently into the hot oil.

6 The ball will puff up and rise to the surface almost immediately. Repeat the process in batches of about 6 at a time. Turn the balls over so that they become crisp and golden brown all around.

7 Remove them with a slotted spoon and drain on paper towels.

8 Transfer to a serving plate while still hot, pour the honey over them, and sprinkle with cinnamon. Serve them immediately.

Note: One can make a lighter syrup by dissolving the honey in water by stirring well, bringing it to the boil, and then allowing it to simmer for about 5 minutes. Can be used hot or cold.

Semolina Halva *(halvas simigdalenios)*

Notes:

– The traditional Greek semolina halva recipe is often referred as "1:2:3:4", as it calls for one cup of oil, two cups semolina, three cups sugar and four of water. This popular pudding is sweetened (unsurprisingly) with syrup and usually studded with nuts and, sometimes, raisins or currants. It is a dessert that has Arabic origins but has been adopted into the Greek culture and is widely served during fasting periods because there are no eggs or dairy products in the recipe.

– As with so many traditional Greek recipes there are several versions with some using orange juice and zest, some using walnuts and/or pine nuts, and that on Lesvos made with flour rather than semolina, and even containing eggs, milk and grape syrup (*petimezi*). Yet another type is called halva Farsalon, named after the town Farsala, in Southern Thessaly in Greece. It is unique in that it's made with corn starch (not semolina) and the consistency is of a jelly with a buttery caramel flavour.

– Then there is the commercial type and the primary ingredients in this confection are sesame butter or paste (tahini) and sugar, glucose or honey. Other ingredients and flavourings, such as pistachio nuts, cocoa powder, orange juice, vanilla, or chocolate are often added to the basic tahini and sugar base. This halva is drier and crumblier than the semolina type.

Ingredients

1 cup olive oil
2 cups coarse semolina
2½ cups sugar (or 2 & ½ honey)
4 cups cold water
½ cup whole or flaked blanched almonds (or other nuts)
½ cup seedless raisins or currants (optional)
1 cinnamon stick
1 tsp ground cinnamon for garnish

1 Start by preparing the syrup. Put the sugar and water into a pan, add the cinnamon stick and over a high heat bring to the boil. Boil until the sugar has dissolved and the syrup slightly thickens. Set aside but keep warm.

2 In the meantime, heat the oil in a large heavy-bottomed saucepan until it is almost smoking hot and add gradually the semolina. Stir continuously with a wooden spoon to allow the semolina to absorb the oil.

3 When the semolina starts to bubble turn the heat down, add the almonds and allow to brown together until golden (whilst constantly stirring). The more you cook the mixture, the darker it will become. So be careful not to overcook it, as the semolina will burn, and the halva will become bitter.

4 Remove the semolina from the stove and, after taking out the cinnamon stick, pour in the warm syrup while stirring with a wooden spoon.

5 Return to a gentle heat and cook the halva (whilst stirring) until the mixture

thickens, look smooth and pulls away easily from the sides of the pan.

6 Remove the pot from the stove, add the raisins if they are being used, and blend. Cover the halva with a towel and let it rest for 10 minutes. Pour the mixture into a pudding mould or into individual bowls.

7 Allow the halva to cool for about 1½ hour before serving so that it becomes easy to slice. Garnish with some cinnamon powder and serve with a side of Greek yogurt or vanilla ice cream.

Note: Although the basic traditional Greek halva recipe doesn't include almonds, it's always a nice addition, which gives extra flavour and crunchiness.

Baked quince *(kidonia psita)*

Ingredients
4 quinces
16+ (approximately) whole cloves
½ cup of Mavrodaphne/sweet red wine
¾ cup sugar
2 cinnamon sticks
2 star anise (optional)
1 orange (juice and zest)
Juice of half a lemon

1 Wipe off the furry coat of each quince and wash them well. Cut them into halves or quarters and core them. Rub each piece with lemon to prevent it going brown, push in one or two cloves, and then place it skin side down in an ovenproof dish with a lid.

2 Add the spices, and after dissolving the sugar in the wine add the orange and lemon juice, then pour this over the quince.

3 Cover with a lid or foil and bake in a preheated oven at 180°C for about an hour or until fork soft, turning the quince and basting occasionally with the juices.

4 The quince can be served hot or cold ideally with some thick Greek yoghurt, whipped cream or ice cream.

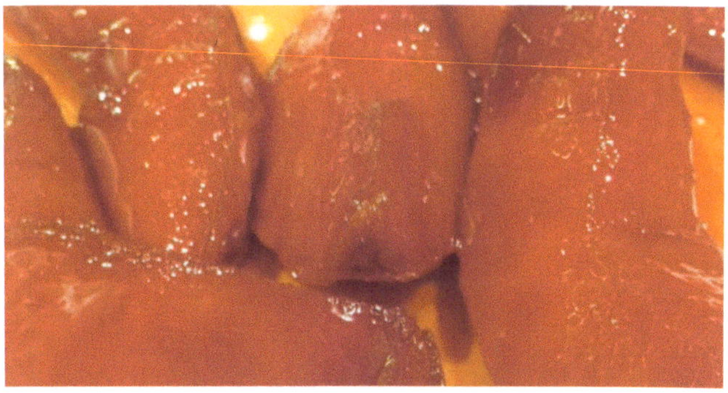

Greek salad *(horiatiki)*

Notes:
– *Horiátiki (saláta)* — which means villager's or peasant (salad), from *horiátiki*, feminine of *horiátikos*, of village-dwellers (or of the peasantry), from *horiátis*, village-dweller or peasant, from *horió*, village — is the summer salad par excellence in Greece.
– Greeks almost always dress a tomato salad with plain olive oil.

Ingredients

2-3 medium sized tomatoes
1 cucumber
1 green pepper
1 onion
Black olives
100 g feta cheese
Dried oregano (rigani)
Olive oil
Salt/freshly ground black pepper

1 Wash the tomatoes and cut them into wedges.

2 Wash the pepper, core it and cut into thin slices lengthways. Slice the onion thinly.

3 Peel the cucumber and cut into medium thick half-rounds.

4 In a bowl mix all the vegetables, add the olives, and dress it all with some olive oil, salt, pepper and oregano. Put the slice of feta cheese on top.

Note: Cos or romaine lettuce is a variety that grows in a tall head of sturdy dark leaves, almost oblong in shape, with firm ribs down their centres. Unlike most lettuces, it is tolerant of heat. The outer leaves are slightly bitter, but the inner ones are sweeter and more delicate. It is often sold as 'hearts' with the outer leaves removed.

Lettuce salad *(marouli salata)*

Notes:
– Cos, the only variety of lettuce grown in Greece, are at their best in the spring as they tend to become rather hard later in the year.
– If one wraps the lettuce in a damp cloth and stores it in the fridge beforehand it is supposed to make the leaves extra crunchy.

Ingredients

1 small lettuce
3-4 spring onions
Some fresh dill
4 tbsp (about) olive oil
2 tbsp (about) lemon juice
Salt/freshly ground black pepper

1 Wash the leaves thoroughly in cold water and drain well in a colander. Allow to dry and then cut the leaves across very finely. It is considered that the finer they are the better the salad.

2 Trim and rinse the spring onions and when dry cut them up quite finely.

3 Cut up the dill and put all the ingredients into a bowl.

4 Mix the olive oil, lemon juice and seasoning separately, then pour over the salad and toss.

Aubergines with *trahana*

Notes:

– *Trahana*, known on Crete as *xinohondros*, is one of the most ancient and delicious foods of Greece and other parts of the eastern Mediterranean.

Basically made with coarsely ground wheat and sour milk, it was used as a porridge or gruel by the ancient Greeks. There are many versions of this product around Greece, some made with fresh milk — usually goat's or sheep's milk — which makes the sweet kind, and some with sour milk (buttermilk) or yogurt to make the sour kind. Until a generation ago it was traditionally the shepherd's and farmer's breakfast, and one of the most common foods of Crete eaten either fresh or after it had dried. It was originally made from left over milk because it was a good way of conserving it as well as the wheat.

– On Lesvos, for example, *trahana* is called *koupes*, which means cups, because of the way it is shaped into little bowls.

– The basic way of making it — almost always during the hot dry month of August — is much the same everywhere. The liquid is poured into a pot, the ground wheat is added, usually with some salt, and the mixture is then boiled over a very low heat, while stirring continuously until all the liquid is absorbed and it is thick enough to be cut with a knife. This is then divided into equal size pieces which are dried in the sun for four or five days. These hard chunks (often broken up into smaller pebbly pieces) if stored in airtight containers, keep almost indefinitely.

– The *trahana* is usually added to soups and stews, or combined with vegetables in various ways, heightening the flavour, and giving every dish it is used in a piquant earthy quality.

– To compare *trahana* to gruel or thickener does not begin to do it justice, conjuring up images of tasteless stodge. Nothing could be further from the truth. While it was thought of as 'poor people's food' until relatively recently, nowadays, as chefs and writers search deeper into their roots and traditions, it is coming into its own and restaurants offering regional specialties have it on their menus. Packets of it can now easily be found on the ever-growing shelves of traditional products and health foods in Greek supermarkets and in Greek delis elsewhere.

Ingredients

1 kg long skinny aubergines washed
½ cup olive oil
2 large onions chopped
2 cloves garlic chopped
2 tomatoes skinned & chopped (or grated)
½ tsp sugar
½ cup chopped parsley
2 bay leaves
1½ cups water (or chicken stock)
1½ cups tarhana
Freshly ground black pepper

1 Remove the stems and cut the aubergines into slices about 2½ cm thick. Soak them for about an hour in a large bowl of salted water to get rid of their bitterness. Squeeze out as much water as possible and dry on paper towel.

2 Heat the oil in a large non-stick frying pan or deep saucepan, and sauté the onions and garlic until they begin to soften.

3 Add the aubergine and continue to sauté, stirring to colour them on both sides.

4 Mix in the tomatoes, sugar, parsley and bay leaves. Stir the mixture well, and let it simmer, covered to coax the liquid out of the tomatoes, over a low heat for 5 minutes. If the aubergines start to stick add a little water or stock.

5 When the aubergines are half done stir in the *trahana* and add 1 cup of water.

6 Cover the pan again and simmer until the liquid has been absorbed and the grains are tender.

7 Check the pan from time to time to make sure they are not sticking and add more liquid as necessary. Season with freshly ground black pepper.

Note: A traditional favourite, homemade *hilopites* are another, and the most common, type of Greek pasta. Though the shape can vary a little from short "linguine" to small squares — a shape that can be easily used in soups, stews and savoury pies — there is no right or wrong. While commercially produced *hilopites* are generally around 1 cm square traditional homemade ones are often made much larger. Frequently served with meaty stews and hearty sauces, it is also enjoyed simply with classic grated cheeses like *mezithra.* Though widely available in stores, *hilopites* are easy enough to make with a simple recipe (see next page), but the process is a bit time-consuming, so one needs to make sure to plan ahead.

Greek pasta *(hilopites)*

See note on previous page.

Ingredients

600 g bread wheat flour
4 eggs
150 ml milk
1 tsp salt

1 In a bowl beat the eggs. Add the milk mixing it all to incorporate. Sift the flour and salt into a large bowl make a well in the centre and pour in the egg and milk. Mix until the dough is slightly sticky but firm.

2 Knead the dough on a well-floured work surface for about 10 minutes or until it is smooth and elastic. Return it to the mixing bowl, cover with plastic cling film to protect from drying, and let it rest at room temperature for an hour.

3 Cut dough into 8 pieces and shape into balls. Taking one ball of dough at a time, roll it out on a well-floured surface to 1-2mm thick (alternatively use a pasta machine). Set aside (on well-floured flat surface) and repeat with remaining dough. Let the dough sheets dry slightly before cutting (about 30 mins).

4 To cut, place the dough in a pile with a good amount of flour between each sheet to ensure they do not stick. Cut sheets into 5-10 mm wide strips (you can use a pasta cutter for fettuccini to do this). The strips can then be cut into 50 mm lengths or if you prefer 5-10 mm squares.

5 Place cut pasta on a clean, flat, floured surface and let dry slightly before cooking it fresh. Alternatively, they can be dried fully which depending on the temperature and humidity could take 5-6 days. Once dry, the *hilopites* can be stored in an airtight container and kept in the refrigerator for six months. Cook as you would any dry pasta in salted boiling water and serve with grated cheese, and your favourite sauces.

Sesame bread ring *(koulouri)*

Note: Many Greeks buy something to eat on their way to work. In short, breakfast (for those that eat it) in Greece is a hurried affair: either a stop at a *Bougatsa* or *Tyropitadiko*, or at one of the many vendors that sell probably Greece's most well-known street food, the *koulouri*.

Ingredients
500 g strong bread flour
1 tsp (8 g) dried yeast
1½ tsp salt
1 tsp sugar
250 ml (approx.) of lukewarm water
3 tbsp oil (sunflower or olive)
200-250 g sesame seeds

1 Dissolve the yeast and sugar in the warm water, cover with cling film and set aside for about 10 minutes until the yeast starts bubbling.

2 Sift the flour and salt into a large bowl and make a well in the centre. Pour the yeast and oil into this and stir or knead until the mixture forms a dough that should be smooth, elastic and slightly sticky. If too sticky add a little more flour.

3 Lightly grease the sides of the bowl, replace the dough, cover with cling film and set aside to prove in a warm place until it has doubled in size.

4 Knock back the dough and knead for a few minutes before dividing it into about 12 equal pieces. Roll these into sausage shapes about 35 cm long.

5 Dip these in water and then roll them in the sesame seeds that have been spread out in a shallow pan or tray before gently forming them into a ring and firmly pressing the two ends together.

6 Lay the rings on a greased baking sheet and bake in a preheated oven at 200°C for about 15 minutes until golden brown.

Appendix 2: Lesvos

Because this book has its roots in the island it seems only right to end with a short description of Lesvos, the third largest island in Greece after Crete and Evia (Euboea). Most Greeks call this rather strangely shaped island, which has been likened to a giant jigsaw piece, Mytilini which is also the name of the capital. The roughly triangular basic shape is cut into very deeply by two great landlocked bays, Kalloni in the south-west and Yera in the south-east, resulting in a shape of great irregularity.

It is a rugged island, with mountains reaching almost to 1000 m in both the north and the south, and large areas of wild, middle-altitude hills in between. Unlike most Greek islands the predominant rocks are not limestone, but mostly volcanic, which denotes crustal instability — an activity by no means extinct as the incidence of earth tremors and the presence of numerous hot springs bear witness. The island's strata have been weathered to produce some fertile soils which has given rise to a beautiful and varied landscape with many features of interest.

Olive growing is the predominant land use, and there are said to be around 12 million olive trees on the island, accounting for about 25% of Greece's olive production. Lesvos produces some of the best olive oil in Greece and has many olive-oil refineries. Fortunately, the olive groves make up a huge wildlife resource, rich in flowers, breeding birds, and mammals, in a landscape of great charm.

As a confirmation of its importance on the island, there are two museums of olive oil. Firstly, The Museum of Industrial Olive-Oil Production that presents the industrial phase of olive oil production in Greece. It focuses on the changes brought about by the introduction of mechanisation. The Museum is housed in the old communal olive press of Aghia Paraskevi, with the buildings and the mechanical equipment restored in an exemplary fashion. Secondly, the Vrana Olive Press Museum originally one of the first steam-powered factories on the island. It operated continuously until the early 1970s, when it closed down and surrendered to the decay of time. In 1999, this industrial monument of unique architectural value came into the possession of the Archipelagos Society (a non-profit organization dedicated to the protection and cultural development of the Aegean) which undertook the work of restoration. At the same time the historical equipment of the factory was also restored and put into operation, granting the visitor an accurate picture of traditional olive-oil production.

In contrast to the south and east, the west is a wild and unspoilt area, with many rare birds, some endemic flowers, and one of the finest fossil forests in Europe that has been designated as a preserved natural monument since 1985. It is a forest ecosystem that was fossilized 15-20 million years ago due to the intense volcanic activity in the area. It included coniferous forests and mainly huge sequoias and primitive pine trees. It is one of the rarest natural monuments in the world (the only similar ecosystems today are the coniferous forests in north America),

and is visited by thousands of tourists. The removal and transfer of fossilized material is prohibited by law. The forest includes six visitor parks in the area. The scenery in this western part of the island is extraordinarily rugged and stony, lacking any high peaks but wild, hilly, and unspoilt almost throughout.

Mitilini is the Capital of Lesvos and of the Prefecture (which has approximately 30,000 residents), and is one of the oldest Greek cities. It is the administrative centre and the seat of Lesvos Prefecture, the Aegean Marine Ministry, the North Aegean Region and

the Aegean University. Not to everyone's taste, it extends over seven hills and the traditional houses coexist with neoclassic mansions, Byzantine temples, refugee neighbourhoods and ancient monuments.

On the north eastern corner of the island is Mithimna, also known as Molivos, about as different from Mitilini as two towns on the same island could possibly be. Mitilini is a working port town, low on sophistication or pretension, with little organized tourism but lots of local character. Molivos with its cobbled labyrinthine streets and castle-crowned hill is a picturesque seaside village, and a truly beautiful place, but in the summer it exists only for tourism due to its remote location.

Also on the north coast is the exceptionally lovely fishing port of Skala Sikaminias, a miniature gem — serene and real, with several good fish tavernas on the edge of the dock. The novelist Stratis Myrivilis used the village as the setting for his *Mermaid Madonna.* Those who have read the book will recognize the tiny chapel at the base of the jetty. The author's birthplace and childhood home are in Sikaminia, the village overlooking Skala Sikaminias — and the Turkish coast — from its perch high above the sea.

The island has several historic towns and charming villages dotted about in its dramatic landscapes. For example Agiassos village, the prettiest hill town, that sits in an isolated valley amid thousands of olive trees, near the foot

of Mt. Olympus, the highest peak. The age-old charm of Agiassos can be seen in its gray stone houses, cobblestone lanes, medieval castle, and local handicrafts, particularly pottery and woodwork.

Due south of Mount Olympus is located Plomari, the only sizable coastal settlement in the south, and the second largest town on Lesbos. It offers scenic appeal as well as the presence of its famous ouzo-distilling industry. The distillers on the island still stick to largely traditional methods of producing ouzo. Also unchanged are their recipes, each one a unique and closely guarded secret but based on grape alcohol, aniseed, water from the island's springs, and other aromatic herbs from Lesvos. It is possible to visit the distilleries and museums of two of the most famous ouzo-producing families (Barbayannis and Arvanitis). At the Barbayannis Ouzo Museum, which is a the better of the two museums, one can see exhibits from over 150 years of the family's history in ouzo making. One can also visit the factory to see how the ouzo is produced and try it or buy some from the shop.

One additional little-known fact about this lesser-visited isle is that it is endowed with a number of natural hot springs found in stunning and remote natural settings. They have been in use for centuries and, according to ancient writings, the Greeks were among first people to use mineral hot springs for health and well-being, dipping in for a soak in healing waters since 500BC. Those on the Gulf of Yera, with a water temperature around 40°C, are the largest and most popular baths on the island with pools for men and women.

Lesvos has an admirably well-organised and well-publicised set of trekking trails in the north and south of the island. These are marked with colour-coded, easy-to-spot signs and cover a wide variety of landscapes. The walks can be taken in sections, or over a few days, stopping off along the way wherever appropriate.

A very attractive and particularly interesting walk in a most enjoyable setting is one that leads to three monasteries and is something of a classic with the locals of the village of Kalloni. The monasteries — Leimonos, Mirsiniotis (actually a convent with connections to Leimonos) and Metochi — are all different. Leimonos Monastery, which is one of the most important on the island, has many religious relics and items of national importance among which are the remains of St. Ignatius, and articles of folk art which are exhibited in the museum. The library of the monastery is also very important, including manuscripts and printed books.

Bird-watching — or 'birding', as the experts call it — is big business on Lesvos. The island is transit point and home to over 279 species of birds ranging from raptors to waders. As a result, Lesvos is attracting an ever-increasing number of visitors particularly in spring. The area around the coastal village of Skala Kolloni, at the head of the Kallonis Gulf, has become well known in recent years as a prime ornithological site where birds can be watched easily, often at close quarters. There is a fine combination of relatively unspoilt coastal and wetland habitats which collectively attract large numbers of birds.

Lesvos, a significant cultural centre during prehistoric times and flourishing economically, commercially and culturally during archaic times, suffered at the hands of invaders and occupiers to the same extent as all other Greek islands. It was conquered by the Persians in 527 BC, captured by Athens, and became a member of the Delian League in 479 BC. It suffered numerous invasions in the following centuries and in 70 BC was conquered by Julius Caesar, the Byzantines, Genoese and Turks followed.

However, through all these vicissitudes the arts retained a high degree of importance. It was the birthplace of the philosopher

Theophrastus, who presided over the Academy in Athens; of the great lyric poet Sappho; of Terpander, the "father of Greek music"; and of Arion, who influenced the later playwrights Sophocles and Alcaeus, inventors of the dithyramb (a passionate choral hymn especially one sung and danced in honour of Dionysus the god of wine and fertility). Even in modernity, artists have emerged from Lesvos: Theophilos, a poor villager who earned his ouzo by painting some of the finest native modern art Greece has produced; novelists Stratis Myrivilis and Argyris Eftaliotis; and the 1979 Nobel Prize-winning poet Odysseus Elytis.

Theophilos, to take one of these, had a very hard life, partially because people made fun of him since he often wore the traditional Greek kilt, the *fustanella*, in public. In spite of this he continued to draw, painting many murals in villages for little payment, usually for a plate of food and a cup of wine. His works are inspired by history, mythology, nature and life. They are distinguished by their primitiveness but also for their expressiveness and their colour combinations. He was eventually recognized as a great folk painter, but unfortunately only after his death. There is a Theophilos Museum — located in Akrotiri in the suburb of Vareia only 4km from Mytilini — which houses 86 of his works.

The island is to this day a spawning ground for innovative ideas in arts and politics.

Appendix 2: Glossary of Foods and Food Terms in Greece

Note: Variations in spelling may be noted, especially the interchange of "d" and "th."
Alati: salt
Amygdala: almonds
Amigdalota: pear-shaped almond confectionery often made on the islands and served at weddings and baptisms.
Anginares: artichokes. Jerusalem or root artichokes are not known in the Greek kitchen; this term refers to the small globe variety.
Anitho: dill
Arni: lamb, the favourite Greek meat and highlight of feasts.
Avgo: eggs
Avgolemono: egg-lemon sauce prepared by adding fresh lemon juice to whisked eggs. The mixture may be used for fish, vegetables, or casseroles.
Bakaliaros: cod, most often referring to the salted preserved cod.
Baklava: famed Mediterranean pastry whose origin may be debatable but whose crispy sweetness is not. Made from many layers of butter-brushed, nut and sugar-sprinkled layers of *fyllo* pastry.

Barbouni: red mullet, a favourite fish usually served grilled or fried. The cheeks and liver are considered special delicacies.
Bechamel Sauce: the sauce's origin is attributed to Louis de Bechamel, (court of King Louis XIV). However, this same sauce - a roux of fat and flour whisked with a liquid, usually milk or cream - was described by Athenaeus in 200 C.E. and widely used in Greek cuisine.
Bifteki: beef patty/burger.
Bougatsa: a sweet pastry with creamy filling and sprinkled with cinnamon and icing sugar.
Bourekakia: a Turkish name covering all the tiny appetizer pastries made from *fyllo* pastry and filled with many different savoury fillings. In Greece they commonly take their name from the filling, for instance *kotopitakia*, chicken; *tyropitakia*, cheese, etc.
Dafnofila: bay leaves
Dendrolivano: rosemary

Diples: folds of very thin deep fried pastry with honey syrup coating.
Diosmos: mint
Dolmades: stuffed vine leaves.
Dolmadakia: with akia being the diminutive, and dolma meaning any stuffed food, this term refers to tiny stuffed foods such as small rolls of cabbage, spinach, or vine leaves or tiny scooped-out vegetables. These are filled with savoury mixtures such as bechamel sauce and cheese or rice with seasonings.
Domates: tomatoes.

Elia: olive
Eleolado: olive oil
Fakki: meatless brown lentil soup, a standby for fast days and a staple soup when meat is scarce.
Faskomilo: sage
Fasolakia: green beans
Fasolada: a meatless bean soup.
Fava: a meze of yellow split pea served hot and thick and garnished with a little olive oil and lemon juice and a sprinkling of chopped raw onions.
Feta: most widely known of all Greek cheeses, firm, crumbly and white and made from goat's or sheep's milk, usually stored in a salt brine.
Fistikia: pitaachios

Fournos: the traditional clay oven that was once part of every Greek house. Today it usually refers to the oven of the local bakery.
Frappe: a popular iced coffee made from instant coffee.
Fyllo: (also spelled *phyllo* or *filo).* Paper-thin pastry that is usually made commercially of egg, flour, and water. Sold in packages of many sheets, it is the basis of many Greek appetizers, pies, and sweet pastries.
Gala: milk
Galaktoboureko: fyllo pastry with a rich custard filling and syrup.
Garides: shrimp
Garifalo: cloves
Gavros: anchovies
Gemista: see Yemisto
Gigantes: giant beans
Glyka tou koutaliou: spoon sweets
Graviera: one of the best Greek cheeses. Made with sheep's milk in some places and cow's milk in others.

Gyros: one of the most popular Greek street food dishes, consisting of meat such as pork and chicken cooked on a vertical spit. The meat is sliced in thin shavings and is then usually placed in a pita bread along with sauces such as *tzatziki* and vegetables such as tomatoes, onions, lettuce, and cucumbers (see photo above).
Halvas: the homemade version is a simple egg and semolina cake over which is poured a hot syrup. The commercial version is a firm paste of pureed nuts and seeds, predominantly almond and sesame, and may be coloured and/or flavoured with chocolate or pistachio.
Hamomili: chamomile

Hirino: pork
Horiatiki (*salata*): the classic Greek 'village' salad.
Horta: general name given to assorted cultivated and wild greens enjoyed by simply boiling, draining, and serving at room temperature with olive oil and a squeeze of fresh lemon juice.
Htapodi (or Ktapodi): octopus
Imam Bayaldi: slowly baked eggplants stuffed with tomatoes and sliced onions and flavored with garlic. Literally "the caliph fainted."
Kafes: coffee. Turkish coffee introduced into Greece and brewed in a long-handled pot called a briki.
Kalamarakia: calamari or squid. Often served fried as a *meze*.
Kanela: cinnamon
Karidopita: walnut cake.
Kataifia: fine shreds of a wheat flour pastry with chopped nuts and sweet syrup.
Kefalotiri and Kasseri: cheeses that are aged and hard and suited to grating. Very similar to the Italian Romano or Parmesan.
Keftedes (or *keftethes*): tiny meatballs. Usually a part of appetizers.
Kiounefe: sweet cheese pie.
Kolokithakia: courgettes/zucchini.
Kolokithokeftedes: zucchini balls.
Kolokithopita: zucchini pie
Koriandroto: coriander
Kotopoulo: chicken
Koufeta: sugar-coated almonds.
Koulouri: sesame coated bread in a ring shape.
Kourabiedes: rich buttery shortbread-type of cookie baked in round halls then liberally sprinkled with rosewater or orange flower water and dusted with icing sugar. Piled in a mound, these are a Christmas specialty.
Krasi: wine
Kreas: meat
Krema: crea***Kremmidia***: onions
Kritharaki: orzo,pasta in the shape of thick rice grains.
Krokos: saffron
Ksidi: vinegar
Kumino: cumin
Kydoni: quince
Ladi (lathi): may refer to any oil, but usually means olive oil.

Ladotyri: hard cheese steeped in olive oil and ripened for minimum of 3 months. Very crumbly and salty it is prepared in large oil tanks and the more it stays in the olive oil, the stronger the taste.
Lahano: cabbage
Lahanodolmades: dolmades made with cabbage leaves.
Latholemono: oil and lemon sauce.
Lathoxitho: a vinaigrette sauce of oil, lemon juice, or wine vinegar plus seasonings.
Lemoni: lemon
Loukanika: is the common Greek word for pork sausage (usually homemade), but in English it refers specifically to Greek sausages flavoured with orange peel, fennel seed, and various other dried herbs and seeds, and sometimes smoked over aromatic woods. Greek sausages are also often flavoured with greens, especially leeks. The word has been used in Greek since at least the 4th century.
Loukoumades: deep fried balls of dough with honey and sprinkled with cinnamon.

Maidanos: parsley
Manitaria: mushrooms
Maratho: fennel
Marouli: lettuce
Marouli salata: lettuce salad

Mastikha: the powdered resin from a small evergreen grown mostly on the Greek isle of Chios. Used for flavouring yeast dough. There is also a liqueur by the same name.
Mayeritsa: the eagerly anticipated soup of lamb entrails finished with avgolemono sauce and enjoyed after the midnight services of Easter Sunday.
Meli: honey
Melitzanes: aubergine/eggplant
Melitzanosalata: a popular appetizer of aubergine (eggplant) seasoned liberally with onion and vinegar.
Melomakarona (or *finikia*)**:** traditional Christmas cookies similar to kourabiedes but flattened and finished with a drenching of honey syrup and a dusting of nuts.

Metaxa: a brandy-like spirit.

Moussakas: eggplant slices layered with tomatoes, cheese, onions, and ground meat finished with a bechamel sauce.
Meze: a simple term to cover the complex array of delicious, usually savoury, small dishes that may accompany drinks. A variety of these dishes may make a whole meal.
Milo: apple
Moschokarido: nutmeg
Mydia: mussels
Nero: water
Ouzo: a spirit distilled from grape residues and flavoured with aniseed.
Pagoto: ice cream
Papoutsakia: stuffed aubergines with minced meat.
Pastitsio: a form of lasagne.
Peperi: pepper
Pilaf: rice flavoured with herbs, and with vegetables, fish, shellfish or meat.
Piperia: sweet peppers
Pites: pies
Pitta: soft, flat bread, shaped into rounds that can be split to make 'pockets' to hold *souvlakia* and/or salads.
Portokali: orange
Prassa: leeks
Psaria: fish.
Psomi: bread
Retsina: traditional wine flavoured with pine resin.
Revithia: chickpeas
Rigani: oregano
Rizi: rice
Rodakino: peach
Rodi: pomegranate
Sfragida: carved wooden stamp – or religious seal – to decorate the top of bread for church. They have a Byzantine cross with the letters IC XC NIKA that are abbreviations for 'Jesus Christ Conquers (or Triumphs).' (See photo on page 176).

Saganaki (or *Tyraki*): any firm cheese cut in squares, dusted with flour, and quickly fried in hot oil and served as an appetizer.
Salata: salad.
Saltsa: sauce.
Sardela: sardines
Selino: celery
Simigdali: semolina
Sfougato: an egg-based dish similar to a crustless quiche. Typically made by combining beaten eggs with grated cheese and plenty of fresh herbs and vegetables.
Siko: fig
Skordo: garlic
Skordalia (or *Skorthalia*): a smooth thick garlic sauce.
Skordopsomo: garlic bread
Soupies: cuttlefish
Sousami: sesame seeds.
Soutzoukakia: spicy meatballs in a tomato sauce.
Souvla: the name of the spit used to roast lamb. (See page 177).
Souvlakia: skewered cubes of lamb with onions, green peppers, and tomato wedges, all marinated then broiled.
Spanaki: spinach
Spanakopita: pie of spinach and feta in fyllo pastry.
Spanakorizo: spinach and rice. A favorite Lenten dish of browned onions, tomatoes, and chopped spinach with water and rice, then cooked till dry and fluffy.
Stifado: a method of cooking used for any meats or game. Literally a stew.
Strapatsada: an omelette with tomato.
Tahini: smooth puree of sesame seeds.
Tarama: fish roe, usually referring to carp roe.
Taramosalata: smooth creamy dip made of roe, white bread or potato, garlic, oil, and lemon juice.
Thymari: thyme
Tiganito: fried
Tourlou: a baked vegetable dish.
Trahanas: pellet shaped pasta made with milk.
Tyri: cheese. The soft cheeses (Mazithra is one) are usually made from sheep's and/or goat's milk and are dried by hanging them in cheesecloth or draining and setting them in wicker baskets. (See photo on page 179).
Tyropita: pie of layered fyllo pastry (or otherwise shaped), filled with cheese.
Tzatziki: a tangy dip of plain yogurt, minced cucumber, and garlic, salt and pepper.
Vassilikos: basil. Traditionally Greek grow basil for good luck and it is often found in a pot on a windowsill. It is believed to chase away irritating mosquitoes. (See page 177).
Vasilopita: made especially for Saint Basil's Day, this sweet yeast bread contains a hidden coin which gives good luck to the receiver. (See photo on page 177).
Vissino: sour cherry
Votana: herbs
Vrasto: boiled
Yemisto: stuffed
Yiaourti: plain natural yogurt.
Yiouvetsi: a combination of lamb, tomato and orzo.
Zahari: sugar
Zimaraki: pasta

Appendix 3: Index of recipes

Note: Aubergine = eggplant; zucchini = courgette.

CPSIA information can be obtained
at www.ICGtesting.com
Printed in the USA
LVHW072353080121
675853LV00038B/1507
9781916242517